ICELAND

DAVID LEFFMAN

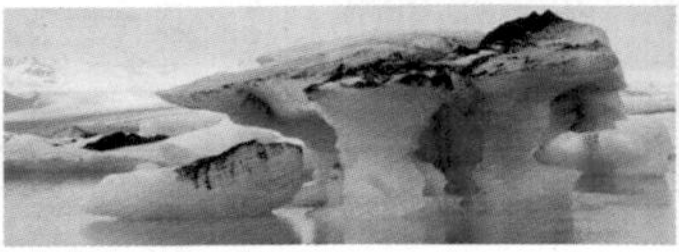

Left **Jökulsárlón** Right **Hot pool at Hveravellir**

LONDON, NEW YORK,
MELBOURNE, MUNICH AND DELHI
www.dk.com

Printed and bound in China by Leo Paper Products Ltd

First published in Great Britain in 2010 by Dorling Kindersley Limited
80 Strand, London WC2 R 0RL
A Penguin Random House Company

14 15 16 17 10 9 8 7 6 5 4 3 2

Reprinted with revisions 2012, 2014

A CIP catalogue record is available from the British Library.

ISBN 978 1 4093 2665 6

Within each Top 10 list in this book, no hierarchy of quality or popularity is implied. All 10 are, in the editor's opinion, of roughly equal merit.

MIX
Paper from responsible sources
FSC www.fsc.org FSC™ C018179

Contents

Iceland's Top 10

The information in this DK Eyewitness Top 10 Travel Guide is checked regularly.

Every effort has been made to ensure that this book is as up-to-date as possible at the time of going to press. Some details, however, such as telephone numbers, opening hours, prices, gallery hanging arrangements and travel information are liable to change. The publishers cannot accept responsibility for any consequences arising from the use of this book, nor for any material on third party websites, and cannot guarantee that any website address in this book will be a suitable source of travel information. We value the views and suggestions of our readers very highly. Please write to: Publisher, DK Eyewitness Travel Guides, Dorling Kindersley, 80 Strand, London WC2R 0RL, Great Britain, or email: travelguides@dk.com.

Cover: Front – **Corbis:** Arctic-Images main; **DK Images**: Nigel Hicks bl. Spine – **Alamy Images**: Jon Arnold Images Ltd. b. Back – **DK Images**: Nigel Hicks tl, tc, tr.

Left **Súðavík** Right **Seltjarnarnes golf course, Reykjavík**

Around Iceland

Streetsmart

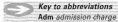

Left **Downtown Akureyri** Right **Skógafoss waterfalls**

Key to abbreviations

Adm *admission charge*

ICELAND'S TOP 10

ICELAND'S TOP 10

TOP 10 Iceland's Highlights

Iceland sits on an active volcanic ridge at the edge of the Arctic Circle, its interior a wilderness of looming icecaps, solidified lava flows and black-sand deserts. Only birds and foxes inhabited the land when Scandinavian Vikings arrived in the 8th century to found the egalitarian Commonwealth of the heroic Saga Age. After 1262, when Norway and then Denmark ruled the country, Iceland fell into poverty, and it was not until the 18th century that towns were established. Today, Iceland enjoys a hi-tech infrastructure and most of its 320,000 population lives around the capital, Reykjavík.

1 Þingvellir National Park

A broad rift valley where the European and American tectonic plates are visibly tearing apart in a riot of geology, Þingvellir National Park was the site of Iceland's Viking parliament *(see pp8–9)*.

2 The Blue Lagoon

Take a sauna or soak in the warm, pale blue waters of Iceland's most sublime outdoor spa, all set among a dramatic landscape of black lava boulders *(see pp10–11)*.

3 Geysir Hot Springs Area

Just an hour from the comforts of downtown Reykjavík, this hillside of violently bubbling pools and erupting water spouts has given its name to similar formations worldwide *(see pp12–13)*.

4 Gullfoss

Huge and powerful, this two-tier waterfall on River Hvítá has been a national symbol since it was saved from oblivion during the 1920s by the first environmental activist in Iceland, Sigríður Tómasdóttir *(see pp14–15)*.

5 Lake Mývatn Area

Lake Mývatn collects the best of Iceland in one place: abundant wildfowl, volcano cones, mud pits, thermal pools and steaming lava flows *(see pp16–17)*.

6 Vatnajökull National Park

This colossal reserve protects not only the central Vatnajökull icecap and its score of out-running glaciers, but also a handful of exceptionally beautiful rivers, gorges and mountain formations *(see pp18–19)*.

7 Snæfellsjökull National Park

Western Iceland's long, snoutlike peninsula peaks with the snowy cone of Snæfellsjökull, a slumbering volcano crossed by hiking trails. It is tall enough to be visible from Reykjavík *(see pp20–21)*.

8 Látrabjarg Bird Cliffs

Fantastically remote even by Icelandic standards, north-westerly Látrabjarg supports one of the largest seabird colonies in Europe, and is home to millions of gulls, guillemots and puffins *(see pp22–3)*.

9 Landmannalaugar Area

Landmannalaugar's bridgeless rivers, shattered grey mountains and hot springs make you feel like an explorer in the wilds. Summer buses make this part of the Interior easily accessible *(see pp24–5)*.

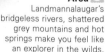

10 Jökulsárlón

Make an easy tour along the Ringroad to this southeastern lagoon between the end of the glacier, Breiðamerkurjökull, and the Atlantic Ocean, full of seals and powder-blue icebergs *(see pp26–7)*.

TOP 10 Þingvellir National Park

Iceland's location on the Mid-Atlantic ridge is obvious at Þingvellir (Assembly Plains) where the land has crashed in a deep scar stretching north from Lake Þingvallavatn. In AD 930, this dramatic setting was chosen by the island's 36 chieftains as the site of their annual Alþing (General Assembly). The country's entire population of 60,000 gathered to hear the laws and to settle disputes, occasionally by combat. The Alþing's power declined after Iceland accepted Norwegian sovereignty in 1262, but the last assembly was held here in 1798.

A view of Law Rock

From the Visitor Centre, through Almannagjá, descend to the Law Rock. Take a detour to see Peningagjá and the church, then walk up to Öxarárfoss. In good weather follow hiking tracks up the rift to abandoned farms, but take care as the dense undergrowth hides deep fissures.

The only place to eat is the café at the Visitor Centre near Öxarárfoss.

- *Map C5*
- *From Reykjavík, Golden Circle tour buses visit Þingvellir daily year-round. Some 2 and 2a buses and summer services using the Kjölur Route also stop. If driving, allow 60–90 minutes via Route 36.*
- *www.thingvellir.is/english*
Bus: www.bsi.is

Top 10 Features

1. Lögberg (Law Rock)
2. Þingvellir Church
3. Almannagjá
4. Volcanic Features
5. Þingvallavatn
6. Flora
7. Visitor Centre
8. Wildlife
9. Öxarárfoss
10. Peningagjá

1 Lögberg (Law Rock)

A prominent outcrop below Almannagjá's cliffs marks the site where the Alþing's Lawspeaker stood and recited the country's laws to the masses below. Look nearby for faint outlines of *buðir*, the tented camps used during Viking times.

2 Þingvellir Church

This surprisingly low-key wooden building with a black roof *(above)*, is a reminder of the Alþing of AD 1000, when, despite strong opposition from pagan priests, the Icelandic nation adopted Christianity as its sole religion. It was built in 1859 but has a 1683 pulpit.

3 Almannagjá

A walk through Almannagjá's deep, cliff-lined gully *(main image)* is a good way to appreciate Þingvellir's geology. Here, as the North American and European continental plates drift apart at 2.5 cm (1 inch) a year, Iceland is literally ripping in half.

4 Volcanic Features

The broad, flattened dome of northerly Skjaldbreiður – an ancient shield volcano – was the source of the lava flow now covering Þingvellir's valley. Cut by deep fissures, the lava cooled into rough a'a outcrops and pavements of smoother pahoehoe (both types of lava).

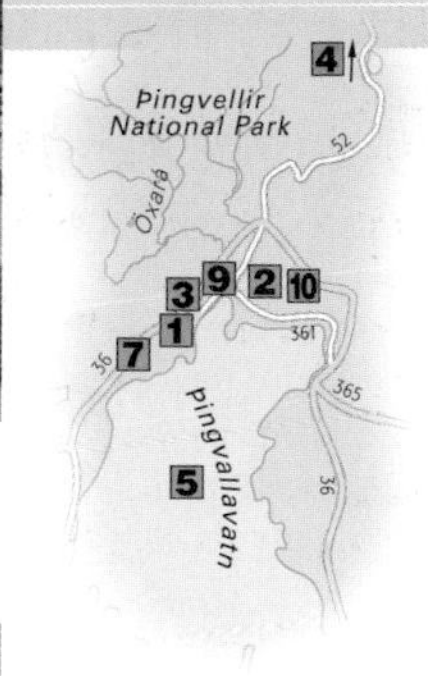

5 Þingvallavatn

At 84 sq km (33 sq miles) Þingvallavatn is the largest natural lake in Iceland. Its clear waters are famous for charr and trout fishing and scuba diving.

6 Flora

Þingvellir valley's floor is covered in a thick carpet of moss, lichen, orchids, dwarf willow and birch. Visit in autumn for exceptional colours and join locals to pick crow-berries (used for jams).

7 Visitor Centre

Perched atop the western side of the rift on Route 36, the Visitor Centre offers superb views of Þingvellir. It also has multi-lingual films and DVDs on the region's geology and history.

8 Wildlife

The area just north of Þingvallavatn's lakeshore abounds in wildlife. Look for swans, mergansers and northern divers on the water and snipe, ptarmigan, mink and Arctic fox on land.

9 Öxarárfoss

Legend has it that the falls were created when Öxará river *(left)* was diverted around AD 930 to provide drinking water during the Assemblies. During medieval times, executions were also carried out here.

10 Peningagjá

Peningagjá is an extraordinary sight: a narrow but deep lava fissure flooded with clear, peacock-blue water. At the bottom of this naturally-created wishing-well you can see the glinting coins.

Paying the Penalty

Lawcourts at the Alþing strangely had no power to enforce their judgments. Litigants accepted the verdicts because they reflected public opinion, but in theory – and sometimes in practice – powerful men could ignore sentences against them. The courts tried to resolve serious disputes through mediation, though the highest penalty in Viking times was not execution but being outlawed – banished from Iceland – for three years.

TOP 10 The Blue Lagoon and Around

The Blue Lagoon (Bláa Lónið) *is Iceland's premier geothermal spa and one of the country's most beautiful. Set in a desolate lava wilderness, the lagoon's bright blue waters add a surreal splash of colour. You can laze in the steaming waters, have a beauty treatment, enjoy an excellent meal or stay nearby and catch the seasonal aurora display. If you have your own transport, consider a detour to see some unusual sights: Grindavík's Saltfish Museum, the Seltún Hot Springs and Selatangar's abandoned fishing camp.*

Shop at the Blue Lagoon

The Blue Lagoon's high mineral content can damage your hair – protect it by rubbing in conditioner before a swim and make sure you shampoo thoroughly afterwards.

Apart from the main restaurant, there is a basic café at the Blue Lagoon's entrance where you can buy coffee, cold drinks and snacks.

- *Map B5*
- *The Blue Lagoon, 240 Grindavík, 420 8800*
- *Several tour buses daily from Reykjavík's BSÍ station. Bus website: www.re.is*
- *Open 1 Sep–31 May: 10am–8pm, 1–30 Jun & 16–31 Aug: 9am–9pm, 1 Jul–15 Aug: 9am–midnight daily*
- *Adm ISK5,300–6,450*
- *www.bluelagoon.com*
- *Icelandic Saltfish Museum: Map B5*
- *Seltún Hot Springs: Map B5*
- *Selatangar: Map B5*

Top 10 Features

1. Background and Origin
2. Unique Lava Setting
3. Public Bathing Pool
4. Spa Services
5. Dermatology and Health Clinics
6. Restaurant
7. Icelandic Saltfish Museum
8. Overnight Accommodation
9. Seltún Hot Springs
10. Selatangar

1 Background and Origin

The Blue Lagoon was created when superheated seawater flowing out of the Svartsengi Geothermal Power Station collected in the surrounding lava *(above)*. Locals discovered that a warm dip cured skin ailments and public facilities opened here during the 1980s.

2 Unique Lava Setting

The lagoon is bordered by rough masses of black lava boulders, which lie piled high around the perimeter, hemming in the powder-blue waters.

3 Public Bathing Pool

The water at 37°C (99°F) is comfortable and the huge pool *(below)* is an amazing place to unwind, with an adjacent sauna.

Visit the Blue Lagoon on your way to the airport.

4 Spa Services

Enjoy a relaxing massage at the lagoon itself, or opt for a cleansing rub-down using the naturally processed fine silica, minerals, algae and salt distilled from the Blue Lagoon's waters. It is a good idea to book spa treatments in advance.

5 Dermatology and Health Clinics

The Blue Lagoon's mineral salts and white clay have long enjoyed a reputation for quickly curing eczema, psoriasis and other skin problems. You can seek specialized treatment at the Clinic *(left)* or simply buy preparations for use at home.

6 Restaurant

Enjoy fine Icelandic dishes such as grilled lobster with garlic butter, fillet of lamb or plain baked fish, with a view of the lagoon right from your table *(below)*. There is also an excellent bar accessible from the water and a café that sells wholesome snacks.

7 Icelandic Saltfish Museum

At Grindavík village, a short drive south of the lagoon, is this eccentric museum that traces Iceland's fishing heritage through dioramas and photographs.

8 Overnight Accommodation

You can stay at the Blue Lagoon Clinic or the Northern Lights Inn – the latter is a fantastic spot in winter, when the colourful aurora borealis play across the night sky.

Seltún Hot Springs 9

Around 22 km (13 miles) east of the Blue Lagoon, a waft of sulphur signals arrival at Seltún Hot Springs *(right)*, a geyser which blew itself apart in 1999. Stick to the boardwalk while exploring the steaming vents.

10 Selatangar

Overlooking the sea 15 km (9 miles) from the Blue Lagoon, this fishing village was abandoned in the 1850s. Ruined walls and foundations are visible through the black sand dunes and lava outcrops.

Geothermal Power

Svartsengi Geothermal Power Station takes advantage of its location over a fault line to provide cheap, green power and heating for Reykjavík. Seawater is pumped over 1 km (0.6 miles) underground, which turns to steam and is used to drive the turbines that help produce 76MW of electricity. The steam is then cooled and released into the Blue Lagoon. Five geothermal plants produce a quarter of the nation's electricity.

TOP 10 Geysir Hot Springs Area

The Geysir Hot Springs area lies on the lower slopes of Bjarnarfell, 90 minutes northeast of Reykjavík, and comprises a dozen or more hot water blowholes, including Geysir, the spout that gave its name to other geysers worldwide. The area became active about 1,000 years ago and today the most impressive spout is Strokkur, which you will definitely see in action. Geysir's pool is far larger but count yourself lucky if you see more than bubbles. Visit Haukadalur for an interesting old church and some undemanding hiking.

People standing beside the hot pools of Blesi

Take great care to stay on boardwalks or marked trails, and do not step into pools or their outflows, as the water is boiling hot. Falling spray from Strokkur is cool, but you will need a raincoat if you are standing downwind.

The Geysir Centre has a café serving coffee, hot dogs, drinks and sandwiches, but the pricier hotel restaurant actually offers better value for money.

- *Map C5*
- *The Geysir area is right by the roadside on Route 35, about 90 min from Reykjavík.*
- *Tour buses are available from Reykjavík's BSÍ station; bus website: www.bsi.is*
- *Geysir hotel website: www.geysircenter.com*

Top 10 Features

1. Geysir Hot Spring
2. Blesi
3. Strokkur
4. Litli Geysir
5. Konungshver
6. Haukadalur Church
7. Hótel Geysir
8. Haukadalur Forest
9. Geysir Centre
10. Bjarnarfell

1 Geysir Hot Spring

Geysir, "the Gusher", *(above)* has not erupted to its full 70-m (230-ft) height since the mid-20th century, though until the 1980s, dumping soap powder into the pool used to trigger a hiccup or two.

2 Blesi

Up the slope behind the Geysir area, Blesi, "the Blazer", is a set of twin pools, one clear and scalding; the other cooler, opaque and powder blue with dissolved minerals *(below)*.

3 Strokkur

"The Churn" *(main image)* reliably erupts every few minutes, its clear blue pool exploding in a 15–30 m- (50–100 ft-) high spout with little noise. In between eruptions, watch the water sighing and sinking as the pressure builds.

Geysir is least crowded before 10am.

4 Litli Geysir

Often overlooked on the walk up to Strokkur, Litli Geysir lies off the path to the left. It was probably once a waterspout that blew itself apart, and is now a small and violently slushing muddy pool, generously belching steam and bubbles.

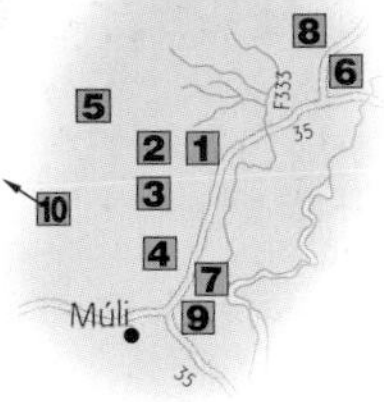

5 Konungshver

Catch the "King's Spring" *(above)* on a sunny day and the colours are stunning. The clear, vivid blue water sits in a depression of orange-red rock. Get views from here of the rest of the Geysir area.

6 Haukadalur Church

In a woodland about 2 km (1 mile) behind Geysir, this church has a door ring said to be given to a farmer by a giant, Bergþór, whose burial mound lies nearby.

7 Hótel Geysir

This hotel *(above)*, right across the road from Geysir, uses the same geothermal water source to fill up its pool and outdoor hot tubs – don't miss the experience of an after-dark soak if you're here in winter.

8 Haukadalur Forest

Since the 1940s, Iceland's forestry service has planted millions of larches, pine and rowan trees in the Haukadalur valley. An easy walking trail passes through a gully full of waterfalls.

9 Geysir Centre

Directly over the road from the hot springs, the Geysir Centre has a souvenir shop *(below)*, a café and an entertaining exhibition on the history and geology of geysers. Do not miss a ride on the Earthquake Simulator.

10 Bjarnarfell

It is a steep hike to reach the 727 m (2,385 ft) summit of Bjarnarfell, the hill overlooking Geysir, but the rewards on a good day are spectacular views of the red-brown rock and green fields surrounding the springs.

There She Blows!

Geysers are formed in deep, vertical, flooded vents known as pipes. The water at the bottom of the pipe comes into contact with hot rock and boils, expanding upwards, while cooler water at the surface of the geyser forms a kind of lid, trapping the rising water, until so much pressure builds up that the geyser explodes skywards. Watch Strokkur and you can clearly see this lid bulging upwards just before each eruption.

TOP 10 Gullfoss

The powerful, two-tier waterfalls at Gullfoss on the Hvítá present a stunning sight, whether part-frozen in winter, in full flood during the spring melt, or roaring away during the long summer twilight. Their setting in a deep canyon adds to the spectacle, as does the landscape of icy peaks and gravel desert immediately north – quite a contrast to the green, spray-fed vegetation closer to the river. Take care at Gullfoss and always supervise children, as paths are slippery and there are no safety railings or warning signs.

Cafeteria at Gullfoss

Visit Gullfoss in winter to see it partly frozen and hidden under spectacular ice curtains; in summer, the afternoon provides the best lighting conditions for photographs.

Make sure you try the traditional lamb soup at the Visitor Centre café – refills are free.

- *Map D4*
- *Daily tour buses from Reykjavík's BSÍ station; bus website: www.bsi.is*

Top 10 Features

1. Origin of Names
2. Geology
3. View from the Top
4. View from Below
5. The Canyon
6. Plaque for Sigríður Tómasdóttir
7. Sigríðarstofa
8. Visitor Centre
9. Souvenir Shop
10. Kjölur

1 Origin of Names

Clouds of rainbow-tinged spray hanging over the cataracts have given Gullfoss its name – the Golden Falls. Hvítá (White River) is named after the light-coloured glacial sediment it carries.

2 Geology

The area's volcanic history can be seen on the cliffs, opposite the viewing platform, with their distinct banded ash layers from separate volcanic eruptions, overlaid with granite *(above)*.

3 View from the Top

The main viewing area and the safest at the falls is the platform on the top of the canyon *(main image)*. Orient yourself and take in the dramatic setting.

4 View from Below

Soaked by spray, you can really appreciate Gullfoss' scale from here: the river drops 10 m (33 ft), turns a right-angle and drops again *(below)*.

The Icelandic word "foss" means "waterfall".

5 The Canyon

The canyon continues downstream from Gullfoss for 2 km (1 mile), through hexagonal basalt columns *(left)*. Follow the walking track along the top, or take a white-water rafting trip.

6 Plaque for Sigríður Tómasdóttir

A commemorative plaque to Sigríður Tómasdóttir *(left)* recalls her successful campaign to save the falls from being drowned by a dam project.

7 Sigríðarstofa

The local exhibition centre, Sigríðarstofa *(below)*, showcases the hardships of traditional life in the area, which is caught between relatively fertile plains to the west and the sterile wilderness of Iceland's frozen interior directly north.

8 Visitor Centre

The roomy cafeteria at the Gullfoss Visitor Centre *(above)* serves a delicious lamb soup. The falls are invisible from here but views show mountains and glaciers.

9 Souvenir Shop

The gift shop at the Visitor Centre has nothing for sale that is specific to Gullfoss apart from postcards of the falls, but it is still a good place to find T-shirts, designer outdoor gear, books on Iceland and lava jewellery.

10 Kjölur

This 160-km- (100-mile-) long route runs north from here across the Interior, traversing the gravel plains between the Langjökull and Hofsjökull icecaps *(right)*.

Saving Gullfoss

In 1907, landowner Einar Benediktsson signed away Gullfoss to be submerged by the construction of a hydro-electric dam across the river Hvítá. Sigríður Tómasdóttir, whose father was involved in the deal, was so incensed that she took legal action against the developers. Although she lost the case, public opinion ran so high in her favour that construction never began and Gullfoss was later donated to the nation as a special reserve.

TOP 10 Lake Mývatn Area

Known as Midge Lake in English, Mývatn's unkind label belies reality: it is a peaceful spread of water east of Akureyri, home to swarms of wildfowl in summer. The surrounding landscape, however, is anything but tranquil, with Mývatn hemmed in by a spectacular mix of extinct cinder cones and twisted lava formations, hot bathing pools, boiling mud pits and screaming volcanic vents. North-shore Reykjahlíð is Mývatn's main settlement, where you can organize tours to local sights and also to Askja Caldera in the barren Interior.

Moss campion

In summer you will need to buy face netting from local stores to protect yourself from irritating – though mostly harmless – swarms of tiny flies. They are worse on windless days.

The Gamli Bærinn restaurant-bar at Reykjahlíð has good coffee, light meals, *hverabrauð* (rye-bread baked in geothermal pits) and smoked trout from the lake.

- *Map F2*
- *Local buses and tours from Akureyri. There is an airstrip at Reykjahlíð.*

Top 10 Features

1. Lake Mývatn
2. Pseudocraters
3. Dimmuborgir
4. Waterfowl Crossroads
5. Jarðböðin Nature Baths
6. Laxá
7. Krafla
8. Hverfjall
9. Askja
10. Námaskarð

1 Lake Mývatn

Spring-fed and covering 36 sq km (14 sq miles), Lake Mývatn was created during volcanic activity about 4,000 years ago. Lava formations *(below)* dominate the northern and eastern sides of the lake, while the rest of the shoreline is marshy.

3 Dimmuborgir

This weird, tumbled mass of indescribably contorted lava formations makes for an eerie hour-long wander on marked paths. Make sure you visit the drained lava tube known as Kirkja (the Church) and keep your eyes open for the rare and endangered gyrfalcons.

2 Pseudocraters

Looking like bonsai volcanoes, pseudocraters were formed from steam blisters popping through hot lava as it flowed over marshland. There are plenty of pseudocrater collections around Mývatn but the best, covered in grassy walking tracks, are at Skútustaðir.

4 Waterfowl Crossroads

Insect lava and algae in Mývatn's shallow waters provide abundant food for phalaropes, swans, divers, Slavonian grebes and 13 species of duck, including the rare Barrow's goldeneye, which breeds in the lake's ice-free areas between May and August.

Bring binoculars for bird-watching.

5 Jarðböðin Nature Baths

Like the Blue Lagoon *(see pp10–11)*, Jarðböðin offers the chance to steam away in the open-air, mineral-rich geothermal waters *(left)*. The views here – west down over the lake and its volcanic setting – are even better.

6 Laxá

Laxá *(below)*, or the Salmon River, drains out of Lake Mývatn's south-western corner and then runs to the sea near Húsavík. Walk along its banks to see harlequin duck tumbling in the rough waters between May and July.

7 Krafla

Located northeast of Mývatn, Krafla volcano last erupted during the 1720s, when its lava nearly consumed Reykjahlíð's church. Víti, Krafla's flooded crater, is bright blue *(main image)*.

8 Hverfjall

This 400-m- (1,312-ft-) high cinder cone is built from volcanic ash and gravel. A well-marked path around the crater's rim offers fantastic views.

9 Askja

South of Mývatn is Askja, an 8-km- (5-mile-) wide flooded caldera. The Víti crater nearby exploded in 1875, causing a virtual exodus of the northeast.

10 Námaskarð

Among a landscape of red clay with yellow and white streaks, Námaskarð is an area of violently bubbling, sulphurous mud pits *(below)*. Take great care as you explore.

Krafla Fires

Earthquakes between 1975 and 1984 opened up a long volcanic fissure at Leirhnjúkur, just west of Krafla volcano, an event that became known as the Krafla Fires. Lava poured out over the plain here, leaving behind a fascinating expanse of still-smoking formations which you can reach and explore on foot from Krafla. It is not for the faint-hearted, as the paths are rough and you need to avoid some dangerously hot spots.

Buy fishing licenses at your accommodation.

Top 10 Vatnajökull National Park

Vatnajökull National Park covers 12,000 sq km (4,633 sq miles), 10 per cent of Iceland's surface, and comprises the Vatnajökull icecap and disconnected areas around its fringes. The long canyons and enormous waterfalls at Jökulsárgljúfur; Skaftafell's high moorland and paired glaciers; Lónsöræfi's wilderness and remains of Lakagígar's catastrophic volcanic event can keep you occupied for days. Hiking, ice-climbing, skidooing and even dog-sledding are among the activities possible within this huge park.

Snipe in Jökulsárgljúfur

Most sections of Vatnajökull National Park are completely inaccessible in winter, closed due to bad weather or lack of buses. Plan a trip between July and mid-August to have the greatest choice of places to visit.

There are few places to eat within the park, so make sure you stock up on refreshments from the nearest town.

- *Map F4*
- *Summer-only buses to Ásbyrgi and Dettifoss from Akureyri; to Skaftafell from Reykjavík and Höfn; to Lakagígar from Kirkjubæjarklaustur and Höfn. Lónsöræfi and Hvannadalshnúkur accessible only to experienced hikers. Tours to Vatnajökull by jeep, dog-sled and skidoo from Höfn.*
- *www.vatnajokulsthjodgardur.is*

Top 10 Features

1. Vatnajökull
2. Glacial Features
3. Hvannadalshnúkur
4. Birdlife
5. Ásbyrgi
6. Lakagígar
7. Skaftafell National Park
8. Jökulsárgljúfur
9. Lónsöræfi
10. Dettifoss

1 Vatnajökull

Europe's largest icecap, Vatnajökull dominates the views inland from the south-west, with a dozen or more glaciers descending off its top as they slide inexorably coastwards *(below)*. At least one active volcano smoulders away underneath.

3 Hvannadalshnúkur

Iceland's highest point at 2,199 m (7,215 ft), Hvannadalshnúkur is a *nunatak* (rocky peak) protruding from Vatnajökull's icecap. You need considerable experience to climb it. On a clear day you can see the summit from Skaftafell.

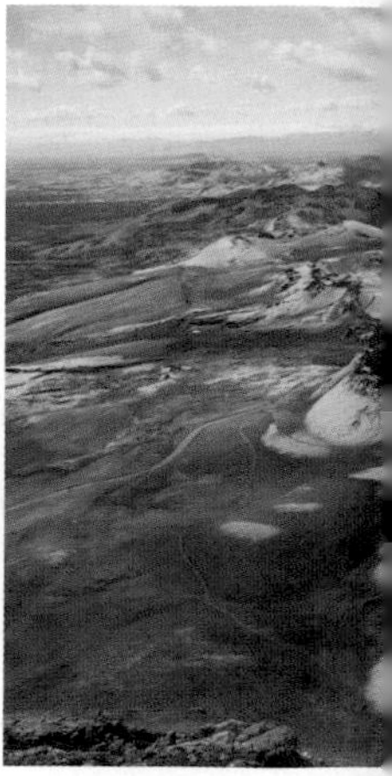

2 Glacial Features

Glaciers are slow-moving rivers of ice advancing just a few centimetres each year (though most of Iceland's glaciers are shrinking). Extreme pressure grinds down underlying rock to leave gravel moraine ridges, and squeezes out the air to give the glaciers their ice-blue colour.

4 Birdlife

Sandar, or deep beaches of black sand washed out from beneath Iceland's glaciers, provide nesting grounds for the greater skua, an aggressive, brown seabird which preys on weaker birds and their young.

"Jökull" means "glacier".

5 Ásbyrgi

This gorge is believed to be an imprint of the Norse god Óðin's eight-footed horse, Sleipnir. Geologists say floods under Vatnajökull carved it *(above)*.

6 Lakagígar

This 25-km- (16-mile-) long row of craters *(main image)* was left by a devastating eruption from Kirkjubæjarklaustur in 1783. Lava and poisonous gas wiped out the farms, causing a nationwide famine.

7 Skaftafell National Park

This park, extending over 1,700 sq km (657 sq miles) of accessible highland plateau, offers superlative hiking along marked trails. Do not miss Svartifoss *(above)*, a waterfall framed by hexagonal granite columns, or the close-ups of blue glacier tongues streaked in gravel.

8 Jökulsárgljúfur

The name of this national park means "Glacier River Canyon", a reference to the 120-m- (394-ft-) deep and 500-m- (1,640-ft-) wide slash through which flows Jökulsá, Iceland's second-longest river *(right)*.

9 Lónsöræfi

This private reserve stretches inland from coastal lagoons through a landscape of fractured orange rhyolite mountains. It can be accessed by hiking.

10 Dettifoss

Said to be Europe's most powerful waterfall, Dettifoss *(left)* sits among a jagged grey granite landscape, its 45-m (148-ft) drop sending clouds of spray skywards. Summer-only access is along a gravel road.

Flash Flood!

Jökulhlaups (glacial flash floods) happen when heat from volcanoes under the icecaps melts enough water to form an enclosed lake. If the lake dam gives way, the water explodes outwards with devastating results. A single prehistoric *jökulhlaup* carved out the Jökulsárgljúfur canyon, while a smaller event in 1996 sent water rushing out from under Vatnajökull, sweeping away 7 km (5 miles) of the highway near Skaftafell National Park.

Snæfellsjökull National Park

Established in 2001, Snæfellsjökull National Park protects the snowy snout of the Snæfellsnes Peninsula, which juts out 70 km (44 miles) into the sea from the western coast. With a beautiful conical volcano at its core, Snæfellsjökull is a place steeped in ancient, literary and New Age folklore, though most people who visit today are more interested in the mountain's hiking or climbing potential. Snæfellsjökull also makes a splendid backdrop for delving into the area's fishing history or bird-watching for rare species.

Interior of Hótel Búðir

To climb Snæfellsjökull you will need ice axes, crampons and weatherproof gear. Talk to the National Park officers at Hellissandur and Hellnar Visitor Centre about your route and weather conditions.

Hellissandur's Café Gamla Rif serves a tasty fish soup.

- *Map A4*
- *Snæfellsjökull National Park's main office: Klettsbúð 7, Hellissandur; 436 6860; open summer only, 10am–6pm*
- *Visitor Centre: Hellnar; 436 6888; open 10am–5pm daily*
- *Buses from Reykjavík to Hellissandur; www.bsi.is, www.west.is*
- *www.ust.is*

Top 10 Features

1. Snæfellsjökull
2. Coastal Boundary
3. Djúpalónssandur
4. Hellnar
5. Dritvík
6. Ascending Snæfellsjökull
7. Bird-Watching
8. Bárður's Statue
9. Hiking the National Park
10. Arnarstapi

1 Snæfellsjökull

Snæfellsjökull is the 1,445-m- (4,745-ft-) high icecap covering the dormant volcano, which last erupted in 250 AD. The white cone of the volcano is clearly visible *(above)* to the north of Reykjavík on a clear day, rising up above Faxaflói Bay.

2 Coastal Boundary

The rugged coast of the Snæfellsnes Peninsula acts as a barrier between the rougher weather to the north and the generally drier, sunnier south. Strong storms with snowfall on the higher ground may occur throughout the year.

3 Djúpalónssandur

A pretty pebble beach *(main image)* near Dritvík where four heavy stones – Useless, Half Strength, Puny and Full Strength – were once used to test the brawn of applicants for fishing boat crews.

4 Hellnar

Hometown *(above)* of an Icelandic woman who travelled widely in the Middle Ages, Guðríður Þorbjarnardóttir. She sailed to Greenland, Rome and America.

*Check the Icelandic Met Office website (**www.vedur.is**) for weather and natural hazard updates.*

5 Dritvík

Some 24 km (15 miles) from Hellissandur, this bay *(above)* harboured what was once the area's busiest fishing fleet. It is a good place to take a break and ponder over changing times.

6 Ascending Snæfellsjökull

Experienced hikers can spend a day climbing Snæfellsjökull. It is also possible to sled up and ski down. However, neither should be attempted without a guide. Get advice from the Visitor Centre or the National Park office.

7 Bird-Watching

Unmistakably large white-tailed sea eagles are often seen in the vicinity of Snæfellsjökull National Park, although this rare bird mainly inhabits the West Fjords. Apart from these, the coastline supports the usual sea birds *(above)* and wild fowl.

8 Bárður's Statue

A terrific split stone statue of folk figure Bárður Snæfellsás stands near Arnarstapi. According to legend, Bárður was an early settler in the area and his protective spirit still lives on Snæfell and watches over the village.

9 Hiking the National Park

Beginning from Hellissandur, a range of circular hiking trails explore the lava fields and coastline west of Snæfellsjökull. Expect to encounter little beaches, rugged seascapes, rare plants, birdlife and seals.

10 Arnarstapi

Set at the foot of Snæfellsjökull's southeast corner, Arnarstapi is a tiny fishing village, where a rocky arch known as Gatklettur stands out to sea. You can also organize snowcat trips onto Snæfellsjökull from here.

Journey to the Centre of the Earth

Snæfellsjökull sprang to fame in Jules Verne's novel *Journey to the Centre of the Earth*, in which a German professor and his nephew decode an ancient manuscript and use the instructions to descend into Snæfellsjökull's crater on a subterranean journey of exploration. Such craters were traditionally feared here as the literal entrances to hell, a belief which left many mountains unscaled till the 19th century.

TOP 10 Látrabjarg Bird Cliffs

The Látrabjarg Bird Cliffs are just about as remote a place as you can readily reach in Iceland. Traditionally a farming area, the region has become almost depopulated since the 1960s, leaving Látrabjarg to the millions of seabirds that return here to breed during summer months. Most people come here to see the abundant numbers of charismatic puffins. On the way there is also a worthwhile folk museum and an amazing beach at Breiðavík, probably the last thing you would expect to find in this part of the world.

Hótel Látrabjarg

The Látrabjarg road is rough gravel, open only in summer. Check your car rental policy before planning a trip. Unless you have experience of similar driving conditions, it is best to take a bus from the capital of the West Fjords, Ísafjörður.

This is a remote area, and the hotel at Breiðavík is the nearest place where you can get a meal.

- *Map A2*
- *Summer-only buses run three times a week from Ísafjörður. Day-returns allow 90 minutes at Látrabjarg; book in advance: 456 5518; www.westfjords adventures.com*
- *Visitor Centre: Egils Ólafsson Folk Museum; 456 1511; open Jun–Sep: 10am–6pm daily*
- *Hnjótur Folk Museum: 456 1569; open 24 May–15 Sep: 10am–6pm daily, by appointment at other times; www.westfjords.is*

Top 10 Features

1. Látrabjarg Cliffs
2. Geology
3. Bird Apartments
4. Eggs
5. Puffins
6. Guano
7. Látrabjarg History
8. Bjargtangar
9. Hnjótur Folk Museum
10. Breiðavík

1 Látrabjarg Cliffs

The 14-km- (9-mile-) long and up to 440-m- (1,444-ft-) high cliffs form a colossal bird colony with millions of seabirds, puffins, cormorants, kittiwakes, razorbills and guillemots nesting here every year *(above)*.

2 Geology

Iceland's western extremity is home to its oldest geological formations. The layered cliffs are a slice through the past, each distinct band – clearly visible despite the birdlife – recording the different volcanic events.

3 Bird Apartments

All the bird species here nest at different heights, forming banded apartments: puffins at the top, then razorbills, fulmars and kittiwakes *(right)*, with guillemots on the narrow sheer cliff ledges.

4 Eggs

Due to their habit of favouring crowded, sheer cliffs, guillemot eggs are conical – a shape which makes them roll in a circle around their tip rather than over the edge.

Látrabjarg has the world's largest razorbill colony.

5 Puffins

The most amiable residents of Látrabjarg are the puffins *(main image)*. These small seabirds have orange feet and a multicoloured, sail-shaped bill. They nest in grassy burrows at the top of the cliffs and often tolerate a cautious approach.

6 Guano

You cannot fail to notice the smell of guano at Látrabjarg. The thick, spongy grass at the top of the cliffs *(above)* exists thanks to the centuries of fertile guano deposits, without which the puffins would have nowhere to dig their nests.

7 Látrabjarg History

The Látrabjarg cliffs were, until 1926, a favourite summer haunt for local farmers, who scaled the cliffs to collect bird eggs. Puffins were once caught and eaten in large numbers, a practice that continues to this day in the southern islands of Vestmannaeyjar *(see p108)*.

8 Bjargtangar

This westernmost point of Europe is marked by the lonely beacon of the Bjargtangar lighthouse, a small, whitewashed and distinctly weatherbeaten building high up on the grassy clifftop. The lighthouse marks the beginning of Látrabjarg cliffs. A warning sign has almost fallen over the edge.

9 Hnjótur Folk Museum

About 50 km (31 miles) from Látrabjarg, this isolated museum provides an insight into the lives of farmers. Do not miss the video of the *Sargon* shipwreck and the aircraft display.

10 Breiðavík

Breiðavík, 15 km (9 miles) from Látrabjarg, features a long, golden beach *(right)* – a rarity here as the sand is usually volcanic black. On a sunny day you could almost imagine yourself in the Mediterranean.

The Wreck of the Sargon

In 1947 a British trawler, *Dhoon*, foundered off the Látrabjarg coast in a December storm. Locals scrambled down the frozen cliffs, fired a safety line onto the stricken vessel and winched the seamen to safety. The following year a film crew arrived to make a documentary about the event when another British vessel, *Sargon*, ran aground: the crew were again saved and the whole event was filmed for real.

Landmannalaugar Area

Landmannalaugar, meaning "Countryman's Bathing Pool," is a lush hot springs area in southern Iceland surrounded by a stark wilderness of snow-streaked mountains, ancient lava fields and flat glacial river valleys. Much of the countryside here has been shaped by Hekla, the country's second most-active volcano. Excellent camping facilities make it a great spot from which to appreciate the rugged interior. It is connected by summer-only buses from Reykjavík. You can also hike here along the exceptional Laugavegur trail.

Horse riding in the Landmannalaugar area

The hot springs can get very busy at weekends and when the Reykjavík bus arrives between 1 and 3pm. If staying overnight, time your soak carefully to avoid the crowds.

In July and early August, you can buy burgers, soft drinks and coffee at the Fjallabúð Café, housed in an old bus at the campsite. There are no other places to eat within 50 km (31 miles).

- *Map D5*
- *Mid-Jun–late Aug: Daily buses from Reykjavík and several a week from Skaftafell. Schedule: www.bsi.is*
- *Open mid-Jun–late Aug*
- *Book bunkhouses at Landmannalaugar and along Laugavegur hiking trail in advance with the Icelandic Touring Club: www.fi.is*
- *www.landmannalaugar.info*

Top 10 Features

1. Hot Springs
2. Mountains
3. Ófærufoss
4. Campsite
5. Laugavegur
6. Ljótipollur
7. Flora
8. Hrafntinnusker
9. Hekla
10. Frostastaðavatn

1 Hot Springs

Hot springs emerge into a meadow from underneath a 15th-century lava flow, where they mingle with a cooler stream. Wade up this stream *(below)* until the water temperature increases, then sit down for a soak.

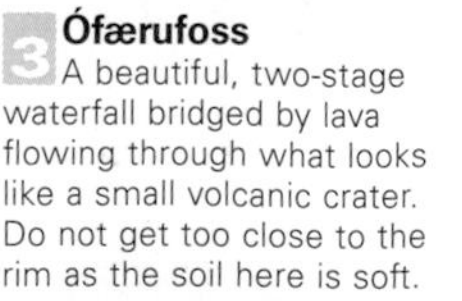

3 Ófærufoss

A beautiful, two-stage waterfall bridged by lava flowing through what looks like a small volcanic crater. Do not get too close to the rim as the soil here is soft.

2 Mountains

The 945-m- (3,100-ft-) high Bláhnúkur is the main peak overlooking the springs, with an hour-long trail to the top. From here you can view the medieval lava field and ever-changing colours of the grey, pink and orange rhyolite hills *(main image)*.

4 Campsite

The spacious campsite *(left)* has some grassy spots on the side of the stream and more pitches on soft gravel. Showers, toilets and a food preparation area are nearby, along with bins of rocks to weigh down your tent against Landmannalaugar's famous gales.

Do not forget to bring a swimsuit and a towel.

5 Laugavegur

This rewarding, 60-km- (37-mile-) long trail *(left)* from Landmannalaugar to Þórsmörk features volcanic plains, green hills, snow-bound plateaus and freezing rivers. You can camp or use bunkhouses along the way while hiking.

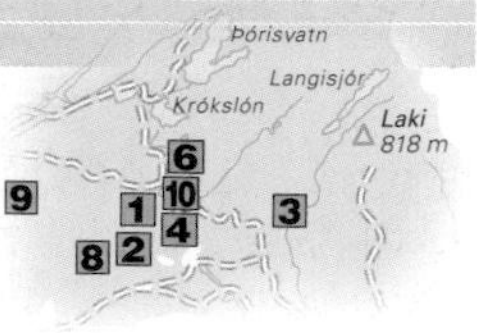

6 Ljótipollur

Do not let the name, Icelandic for "ugly puddle", put you off visiting this small crater lake, which forms an attractive blue pool sunk inside a bright red scoria depression.

7 Flora

Look for tiny, hardy flowers contrasting with the dark lava walls near the springs. Pink thrifts, moss campion, purple self-heal, aromatic thyme, white cottongrass *(below)* and violet butterworts are common.

8 Hrafntinnusker

Hrafntinnusker is a huge "reef" made of obsidian, black volcanic glass, located southwest of Landmannalaugar. Look for weathered outcrops among the lava field and on Bláhnúkur, along with smaller pebbles all over.

9 Hekla

The Hekla volcano, towering 1,488 m (4,882 ft) over southwest Iceland, has been going off at 10-year intervals. The road to Landmannalaugar traverses ash dunes and lava fields from the 1970 eruption *(see p113)*.

10 Frostastaðavatn

Packed with trout, this lake *(below)* around 5 km (3 miles) from Landmannalaugar is a favourite fishing spot. You can hike around the shore in 3 hours, a fairly easy walk except for a stretch over a lava field.

Hiking Laugavegur

The Laugavegur hike isn't especially difficult but you do need to be self-sufficient and prepared against possible bad conditions. Wear warm, weatherproof clothing and hiking boots, carry maps and a compass, and bring your own food as there are no stores along the way. Bunkhouses must be booked in advance. Campsites are laid out at about 15 km (9 mile) intervals and campers need strong tents in good condition along with cooking gear.

TOP 10 Jökulsárlón

Jökulsárlón is a broad lagoon on the southeastern coast, where the nose of the Breiðamerkurjökull glacier edges down to the sea. The lagoon formed after the glacier began receeding during the 1940s and today presents a striking scene, filled by a mass of icebergs freshly broken off the glacier. With a deep, black-sand beach behind you and the white mass of Europe's largest icecap, Vatnajökull, on the horizon, Jökulsárlón is a great spot to stretch your legs on the long drive from Vík to Höfn.

Close-up of glacier ice

All buses travelling along the south coast stop at Jökulsárlón for around 30 minutes, which is long enough to take in the lagoon and walk down to the sea to look at the ice boulders.

The café at the Visitor Centre opens 9am–7pm through summer and 10am–5pm the rest of the year, serving inexpensive hot food, snacks and coffee.

- *Map G5*
- *Visitor Centre: 478 2222; open 15 May–15 Sep; call ahead for boat tours as timings vary*
- *www.randburg.com/is/jokulsarlon*
- *www.vatnajokulsthjodgardur.is*
- *www.jokulsarlon.is*

Top 10 Features

1. The Lagoon
2. The Beach
3. Icebergs
4. Vatnajökull
5. Aquatic Life
6. Breiðárlón
7. In the Movies
8. Birds
9. Visitor Centre
10. Boat Tour

The Lagoon 1

Around 5 km (3 miles) across and fairly narrow, it is the deepest lagoon in Iceland *(main image)*. By contrast, its outflow, the Jökulsá, is the country's shortest river.

3 Icebergs

The pale blue icebergs create a natural sculpture exhibition *(above)*, constantly changing shape as they melt, breaking into smaller floes. Eventually they are small enough to float to the sea.

2 The Beach

Over the highway, it is just a short walk to where translucent, weirdly-shaped boulders of ice – the smaller, depleted remains of Jökulsárlón's icebergs – wash downstream to the sea. There they get stranded on the black-sand beach, making for some evocative photographs.

4 Vatnajökull

The lagoon is a good spot to get a feel for Vatnajökull's vast size *(left)*; Breiðamerkurjökull is 15 km (9 miles) across but even this is only a fraction of the massive white icefield before you *(see pp18–19)*.

5 Aquatic Life

Jökulsárlón's cool, deep waters attract herring and trout, which in turn make it a good place to see seals – often spotted snoozing on ice floes *(above)*. Mighty orca or killer whales also visit on occasion.

9 Visitor Centre

Jökulsárlón's small Visitor Centre *(right)* has a café selling fast food and hot drinks, and a few shelves of souvenir postcards and T–shirts. Climb the black hillock out front for great views of the lagoon.

10 Boat Tour

For a chance to enter the maze of icebergs right up against the glacier snout, take the 30-minute amphibious boat tours *(below)* at the Visitor Centre. With luck you might also get close to the seals.

6 Breiðárlón

For similar scenery but a far more remote atmosphere, head to Breiðárlón, which is 6 km (4 miles) west of Jökulsárlón along the highway and then 3 km (2 miles) north on a gravel road.

7 In the Movies

Movie buffs may well have seen the area even before they visit since Jökulsárlón has featured in two Bond films, a Tomb Raider and a Batman film. It is also a popular place to shoot Icelandic TV commercials.

8 Birds

Bird lovers should look out for the ground-nesting Arctic terns *(above)* and the bulkier brown Arctic skuas. Both have a habit of dive-bombing anything that gets too close to their nests.

Bridging the Rivers

Bridging the numerous deep, ever-shifting glacial rivers which thread their way seawards all along the south coast was such a massive undertaking that the national highway around the country – the Ringroad – got completed only in 1974. Before this, places like Jökulsárlón were well off the beaten track, as the main road between Skaftafell and Reykjavík was, in reality, just a gravel track.

Left **Þingvellir, site of Iceland's first Parliament** Right **Ólafur Tryggvason**

Moments in History

1 AD 860: Viking Exploration
Around this time a Viking named Naddoður discovered an uninhabited coastline north-east of the Faroe Islands. This new land was later visited by Norseman Flóki Vilgerðarson, who, having spent a harsh winter here, named it "Ísland" (Iceland).

Viking explorer Naddoður discovers Iceland

2 AD 870: Reykjavík Settled
Norwegians Ingólfur Arnarson and Hjörleifur Hróðmarsson set sail for Iceland with their families. Hjörleifur was murdered by his slaves after he settled at Hjörleifshöfði. Ingólfur became Iceland's first permanent settler, building his homestead at a place he named Reykjavík (Smoky Bay).

3 AD 930: Alþing Established at Þingvellir
All available land in Iceland was settled by AD 930 and regional chieftains found it necessary to form a national government. Rejecting the idea of a king, they opted for a Commonwealth. The Parliament (Alþing) was convened annually at Þingvellir, where laws were made and disputes settled.

4 AD 1000: Iceland Becomes Catholic
The majority of Iceland's original settlers believed in Norse gods. During the 10th century, however, Norway's king Ólafur Tryggvason threatened Iceland with invasion unless it converted to Christianity. Accordingly, the Alþing of AD 1000 adopted Catholicism as Iceland's official religion.

5 1262: The Old Treaty with Norway
During the 13th century, power moved into the hands of wealthy landowners, who plunged the island into civil war. Norway stepped in as peacemaker, and in 1262 Iceland accepted Norwegian sovereignty as a semi-independent state under the Old Treaty.

6 1397: Denmark Takes Over
Denmark's ruler, the "Lady King" Margrete, absorbed the Norwegian throne under the Kalmar Union. Later on, Denmark rejected Iceland's claims of autonomy, and in 1661 used military force to impose absolute rule.

7 1550: Iceland Becomes Lutheran
The Danish king appointed Gissur Einarsson as Iceland's first Lutheran bishop in 1542. As the nation reluctantly adopted the new faith, Iceland's last Catholic bishop, Jón Arason, took up arms. He was defeated at Skálholt and executed on 7 November 1550.

 Preceding pages **Víti crater lake, Mývatn**

8 **1783: Lakagígar Eruption**
A major volcanic eruption along the Laki craters flooded southeastern Iceland with lava. Poisonous fallout then wiped out agriculture across the land. Famine over the next three years killed one in three Icelanders, and Denmark considered evacuating the entire country to Jutland.

9 **1874: The Nationalist Movement**
The mid-19th century saw a swelling of nationalism in Iceland and a challenge to Denmark's authority. The movement was led by poet Jónas Hallgrímsson and historian Jón Sigurðsson. This culminated in the Danish king Christian IX ratifying a new constitution in 1874, which returned legislative power to the Alþing.

10 **1944: Iceland Declares Independence**
Denmark's invasion by Nazi Germany in 1940 nullified its territorial rule over Iceland, and the Alþing decided to declare independence. Political squabbles confused the process but on 17 June 1944 the country's first president, Sveinn Björnsson, proclaimed Icelandic Independence at Þingvellir, marking the end of 700 years of foreign rule.

Line of Lakagígar craters

Top 10 Figures in Icelandic History

1 **Flóki Vilgerðarson**
The Viking who named Iceland and was known as Hrafna-Flóki, or Raven-Flóki, after his pet birds.

2 **Ingólfur Arnarson**
Iceland's first official settler, who left his native Norway following a feud with the local earl.

3 **Leifur Eiríksson**
Son of Eirík the Red, Leifur sailed west from Greenland in 1000 and discovered America.

4 **Guðríður Þorbjarnardóttir**
Mother of the first European born in North America, she later made a pilgrimage to Rome.

5 **Snorri Sturluson**
The 13th-century historian, politician and author of *Egil's Saga*, the *Heimskringla* and the *Prose Edda*.

6 **Jón Sigurðsson**
Leader of the independence movement, he promoted the move for Iceland's political autonomy from Denmark.

7 **Jónas Hallgrímsson**
Influential Romantic poet who shaped nationalist pride during the 1800s.

8 **Hannes Hafsteinn**
Iceland's first Home Minister in 1904, who oversaw a period of modernization and social change.

9 **Vigdís Finnbogadóttir**
Iceland's president from 1980 until 1996, and the first democratically elected female head of state.

10 **Jóhanna Sigurðardóttir**
The world's first gay political leader, who became the prime minister of Iceland in January 2009.

Left **Gullfoss** Right **Camp at the foot of Dynjandi falls**

TOP 10 Waterfalls

1 Dettifoss

Europe's biggest waterfall in terms of volume, this monster at Jökulsárgljúfur National Park in northeastern Iceland can be heard miles away. The stark setting, where the river drops 45 m (148 ft) between the shattered cliffs of the Jökulsá canyon, adds to the spectacle. Upstream is another fall, Selfoss, only 10 m (33 ft) high but 70 m (230 ft) across. *Map F2*

2 Glymur

Iceland's tallest waterfall, Glymur drops nearly 200 m (658 ft) off the top of a plateau inland from Hvalfjörður, along the west coast. Legend has it that a mythical beast, half man and half whale, swam up the waterfall and into Hvalvatn, the lake at the top – where whale bones have indeed been found. *Map C4*

3 Gullfoss

This large, beautiful and always impressive two-tier fall sits on the River Hvítá around 75 km (47 miles) northeast from Reykjavík. It is one of Iceland's most visited sights, along with nearby Geysir and Þingvellir. In the early 20th century it was at the heart of the country's first environmental dispute *(see pp14–15)*.

4 Seljalandsfoss

Fed by the melting water from Eyjafjallajökull icecap, Seljalandsfoss is narrow and not especially tall, but drops into a meadow along the south coast with surprising force. The path behind the water curtain is muddy and slippery, and a walk along this provides for a good soak. Look out for several smaller falls nearby. *Map D6*

5 Hraunfossar & Barnafoss

Two adjacent falls within easy reach of Borgarnes on the west coast, with very different characters. At Hraunfossar, blue water splashes out from under a

Streams splashing down a moss-covered bank, Hraunfossar

moss-covered lava bank and gurgles down into the river, while Barnafoss forms a short, savage set of rapids as it cuts through a narrow canyon just upstream. ⊗ *Map C4*

6 Skógafoss

Just walking up along the river to this mighty waterfall is an incredible experience: as you approach, the flat gravel plain vanishes inside soaking clouds of spray and a deafening level of noise. Climb a staircase up to the top for more cascades and views out over southern Iceland's coastline. ⊗ *Map D6*

7 Dynjandi

This pretty tumble in the West Fjords near Hrafnseyri cascades over several tiers of granite boulders in a 60-m- (198-ft-) wide, 100-m (329-ft) drop. Crashing over all those boulders gives Dynjandi (the Thunderer) its name, but views seawards over grassy dales make it a beautiful place to camp out. ⊗ *Map B2*

8 Goðafoss

Located between Akureyri and Mývatn, this "Waterfall of the Gods" is where the 10th-century lawspeaker Þorgeir Ljósvetningagoði, who championed the introduction of Christianity to Iceland, disposed of the statues of pagan Norse gods in 1000. The ice-blue water channels over several falls, with easy walking tracks between them. ⊗ *Map E2*

9 Aldeyjarfoss

Off the northern end of the rugged Sprengisandur Route

Skógafoss

across Iceland's interior, Aldeyjarfoss cuts a rough scar across the huge Suðurárhraun lava field, exposing layers of ash and rock settled over successive eruptions. Although only 20 m (66 ft) high, the falls are very forceful and perk up an otherwise lifeless terrain. ⊗ *Map E3*

10 Ófærufoss

This waterfall is associated with the Eldgjá canyon on Fjallabak Route between Landmannalaugar and Skaftafell. The river flows along the top and drops into the canyon, gouging out a broad, scree-ridden pool before falling again as a smaller curtain on to the plain. ⊗ *Map E5*

Left **Arctic skua** Centre **Whale-watching vessel** Right **Látrabjarg cliffs**

Top 10 Places to See Birds and Wildlife

1 Lake Mývatn

The country's top venue for viewing wildlife, Lake Mývatn slots easily into a trip to see Iceland's laid-back northern capital, Akureyri, and a whale-watching expedition from Húsavík. Ducks and other wildfowl are the main draws, but the elusive Arctic fox and gyrfalcon are also regularly encountered *(see pp16–17)*.

2 Látrabjarg

Way out in the West Fjords, a trip to Látrabjarg takes a little bit of planning but you will not forget your first sight of these cliffs, covered by enormous, noisy colonies of nesting seabirds. Stop along the way for a walk or sunbathe on Breíðavík Beach *(see pp22–3)*.

3 Hornbjarg

At 533 m (1,749 ft), Hornbjarg is the highest clifftop on the isolated, completely uninhabited Hornstrandir Peninsula, on the West Fjords' extreme northwest. Like Látrabjarg, it is teeming with millions of fulmars, kittiwakes, razorbills and guillemots, but to get here you will have to catch irregular boats from Ísafjörður and then hike back over several days. *Map B1*

4 Dyrhólaey

The grassy, sculptured headland of Dyrhólaey is an easy detour off the highway between Skógar and Vík. Apart from close encounters with puffins and other seabirds, come here to view the black, volcanic-sand beaches and the huge sea arch, large enough for a ship to sail through. *Map D6 • Closed 1 May–25 Jun*

Razorbill at the Látrabjarg cliffs

5 Jökulsárlón

One of the most spellbinding sights of southeastern Iceland, this deep, iceberg-filled lagoon between the sea and Breiðamerkurjökull glacier is a great place to spot seals and orca, if you are lucky. The sandy plains on either side are full of nesting terns and skuas – and Arctic foxes looking for a meal *(see pp26–7)*.

6 Skjálfandi

A summer sailing trip out from Húsavík to Skjálfandi, the broad bay offshore, is certain to put you within viewing range of marine mammals. You are most likely to see seals and dolphins but with luck you will encounter the spectacular humpback whales leaping out of the water. *Map E2*

The elusive Arctic fox

Tiny islands in Breiðafjörður

7 Breiðafjörður

The waters off the west coast are dotted with hundreds of islets and skerries inhabited by thousands of puffins, shags, cormorants and other seabirds. White-tailed sea eagles, one of Iceland's rare and majestic birds, are also seen here. *Map B3*

8 Garðskagi

Close to Keflavík International Airport, this little tongue of land overlooks a gravelly beach where you can easily spot redshank, sanderlings, turnstones, eider duck and other shorebirds – look out to sea for gannets. The striped red lighthouse was once used to monitor bird migration. *Map B5*

9 Ingólfshöfði

This narrow, sandy spit of land between Vík and Höfn is said to be where Iceland's first settler, Ingólfur Arnarson, landed. Fearless puffins and greater skua nest here in summer, when tractor tours trundle out from the highway. *Map F5 • Hofsnes Farm • 894 0894 • Tractor tours: Apr–Oct daily at 9am, noon & 3pm; book online at www.localguide.is • Adm*

10 Þjórsárver

This extensive expanse of protected, mossy wetland along Iceland's largest river, the 230-km- (143-mile-) long Þjórsá, is where most of the world's pink-footed geese raise their young. Whooper swan, snipe and greylag geese live alongside. *Map E4*

Top 10 Icelandic Birds

1. **Puffin**
   This charismatic bird nests in burrows on grassy sea cliffs around Iceland between May and September.
2. **Arctic Tern**
   A small, graceful seabird which fearlessly dive-bombs anything which gets too close to its nest.
3. **Gyrfalcon**
   A rare, grey-white falcon which once featured on Iceland's coat of arms. Seek them out around Mývatn.
4. **Golden Plover**
   Common grassland bird whose piping call is eagerly awaited by Icelanders as heralding the spring.
5. **Raven**
   Huge black crow with a harsh call and acrobatic flight, considered highly intelligent by many Icelanders.
6. **Meadow Pipit**
   The island's most abundant bird is a sweet songster, though it can be surprisingly hard to see.
7. **White-tailed Sea Eagle**
   Once persecuted by farmers as a pest, around 80 white-tailed sea eagles now breed in the northwest.
8. **Eider Duck**
   Pied sea duck known for its soft, warm down. It is common around the coast and on lakes inland.
9. **Ptarmigan**
   Grouse renowned for its unique, snow-white winter plumage. A popular Christmas dish in Iceland.
10. **Harlequin Duck**
    Sea duck with an unmistakable blue and red plumage. It breeds inland from May to July around fast-flowing streams.

Left **Greens at a Reykjavík golf club** Right **Borgarnes**

TOP 10 Places to Play Golf

1 Hólmsvöllur

An 18-hole, par-72 course on Iceland's westernmost peninsula, Hólmsvöllur is famous for its sunset views and birdlife. It is a challenging course overall, but the 3rd hole is Iceland's most notorious, requiring a 200-m (660-ft) drive over the sea. *Map B5 • Suðurnes, 232 Keflavík • 421 4100 • Adm • www.golf.is/gs*

2 Garðabær

There are three golf courses in Reykjavík's Garðabær suburb, including the 18-hole, par-71 Urriðavöllur and Ljúflingur's easier 9-hole, par-3 course. They are open quite late (until 10pm) through June and July, taking advantage of the long daylight hours. *Map P6 • Urriðavöllur, Garðabær • 565 9092 • Adm • www.oddur.is, www.midnightgolf.is*

Putting at a course in Garðabær

3 Korpúlfsstaðir

Tailored into what was once the sprawling Korpúlfsstaðir farmstead, "Korpá" is an 18-hole, par-72 course set in splendid scenery. Half of the well-wooded course is played along the seafront with Reykjavík's Esja plateau rising beyond, while the rest follows the banks of the Korpá river. The 12th and 15th holes are the toughest. *Map Q5 • Korpúlfsstaðir, 112 Reykjavík • 585 0200 • Adm • www.grgolf.is/english*

4 Keilir

This club, located 30 km (19 miles) from Reykjavík among Hafnarfjörður's extensive lava fields, is named after the distinct conical mountain rising behind it. Hvaleyrarvöllur, the main 18-hole green is rated par-71, with strong winds from the Atlantic as perhaps the biggest hazard – you need accuracy here, not just power. There is also a 9-hole practice course. *Map B5 • Steinholti 1, 220 Hafnarfjörður • 565 3360 • Adm • www.keilir.is*

5 Borgarnes

If the golfing options near Reykjavík are too crowded, drive an hour along the west coast to Borgarnes town and its 18-hole, par-71 green, Hamarsvöllur. It is nicely landscaped, with plenty of natural water hazards, and the distant hills framing the course add to its charm. *Map B4 • Hamarsvöllur, 310 Borgarnes • 437 1663 • Adm • www.golf.is/gb*

All golf courses in Iceland are open to the public: **www.golf.is**

Golfers at the Akureyri greens

6 Akureyri

The world's most northerly 18-hole course, Akureyri's par-71 green is set in wild, open moorland, though stands of trees and rocky outcrops are used to break up the terrain. The annual Arctic Open is held here in June, with tee-offs after midnight against the glowing midsummer night skies. *Map E2 • Jaðar, 600 Akureyri • 462 2974, 896 6814 • Adm • www.gagolf.is (Icelandic only), www.arcticopen.is*

7 Fljótsdalshérað

A popular 9-hole, par-68 course in the suburb of Fellabær, Fljótsdalshérað hosts the East Iceland Open in July. Ormurinn, a giant, snake-like monster, is said to inhabit adjacent Lögurinn lake. *Map G3 • Fljótsdalshérað, Fellabær, 700 Egilsstaðir • 471 1113 (summer only) • Adm • www.golf.is/gfh*

8 Vestmannaeyjar

Founded in 1938, this 18-hole, par-70 course is one of the most dramatic. To the north are the steep, grassy slopes of a collapsed volcano cone; westwards, the green drops into the sea; while to the east is the Eldfell volcano, still steaming after its 1973 eruption. The Volcano Open is held here in July. *Map C6 • Heimaey, Vestmannaeyjar • 481 2363 • Adm • golf@eyjar.is*

9 Krossdalsvöllur

As if there wasn't enough to do around Mývatn – birdwatching, volcano climbing, visiting hot pools and boiling mud pits – there is this 9-hole, par-33 course too. Apart from the hazards, try not to confuse bird eggs for lost golf balls. *Map F2 • Stekkholti, 660 Mývatn • 856 1159 • Adm • stekkholt@emax.is*

10 Geysir Golf Course

Opened in 2006, just a long tee shot from the famous hot springs, this L-shaped, 9-hole, par-37 course is gaining a reputation as one of the best-designed in the country, landscaped carefully using the natural vegetation. The club also sports a driving range. *Map C5 • Haukadalur, 801 Selfoss • 486 8733 • Adm • www.geysirgolf.is*

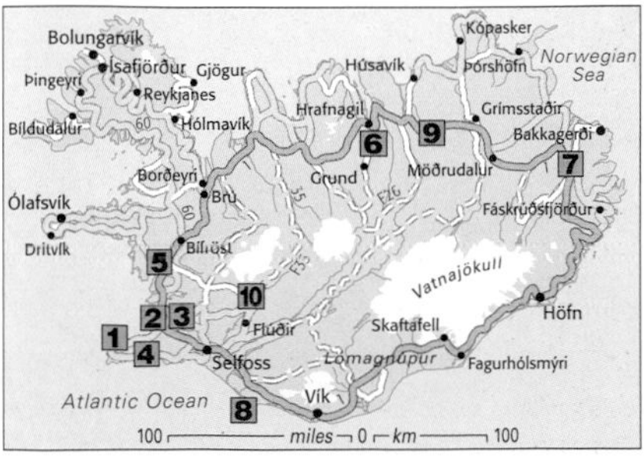

Country greens are cheaper.

Left **Snæfellsjökull icecap, Snæfell** Right **Crater lake, Lakagígar**

Volcanoes

1 Hekla

This large, lively mountain has erupted over a dozen times since Settlement, most famously burying a host of nearby Viking farms under ash in 1104. The last major stirrings were in the 1940s, but there have been many smaller incidents since then. In between eruptions, experienced hikers can walk to the top *(see p113)*.

2 Eyjafjallajökull

In March 2010, an eruption of the Eyjafjallajökull volcano began at the Fimmvörðuháls hiking trail *(see p56)*. A month later, as it petered out, a much bigger eruption started in the main crater. From the 4th until the 20th April, a vast cloud of volcanic ash spread across large areas of Europe. Many countries closed their airspace, affecting hundreds of thousands of passengers. A visitor centre at the base of the volcano, at Þorvaldseyri, shows films of the eruption. *Map D6*

3 Snæfell

This stratovolcano – one whose cone has built up gradually over successive eruptions – is believed to have last erupted around AD 250 and today is covered by the Snæfellsjökull icecap *(see pp20–21)*. Unlike Hekla, whose top is usually shrouded by cloud, Snæfell's bright white peak stands like a beacon over the west coast. *Map A4*

4 Öræfajökull

Iceland's tallest volcano is located near Ingólfshöfði. Its terrible explosion in 1362 buried almost a third of the country under gravel and forced the abandonment of farms all along the south coast. Another eruption in 1727 caused less damage, mainly because only a few people had returned to live here. *Map F5*

Icelandic ponies grazing near Eyjafjallajökull

5 Lakagígar

In 1783, the countryside inland from Kirkjubæjarklaustur split open a huge rent, which belched fire and poisonous fumes for seven months. It is said that Kirkjubæjarklaustur itself was saved by the actions of pastor Jón Steingrímsson, who bundled the town's population into the church and prayed that they be spared – the lava halted right at the church boundary *(see p114)*.

6 Eldfell

The 1973 eruption of Eldfell on Heimaey, in the Westman Islands, buried a third of the town under lava and the rest under ash. But the harbour was saved – and even improved – by the spraying seawater on to the lava front as it edged down from the volcano. *Map C6*

7 Katla

This dangerous volcano lies buried beneath the Mýrdalsjökull icecap near Skógar on the south coast. It erupts on average at a 70-year interval, and the last one, in 1918, sent a titanic flood of meltwater and gravel down nearby valleys. Recent activity in the area, including earthquakes in the caldera, might be signalling an awakening. *Map D6*

8 Grímsvötn

Currently Iceland's most active volcano, Grímsvötn smoulders away 400 m (1,315 ft) below the massive Vatnajökull icecap. A massive *jökulhlaup* – a volcanically induced flash flood – tore out from under the Skeiðarárjökull in 1995, destroying several bridges. There was another eruption in May 2011. *Map E4*

9 Krafla

The Krafla Fires of 1975–84, northeast of Mývatn, happened at a bad time: they delayed the completion of the Leirbotn Geothermal Power Station, under construction at the time, for over a decade. However, the new source of natural heat might make it possible to increase the station's projected 60 MW output *(see p17)*.

Hot pool at Krafla's base

10 Askja

During the winter of 1875, an apparently small vent in the massive Askja caldera exploded with such force that it vapourized two cubic kilometres of rock, which fell as a thick layer of pumice all across northeastern Iceland. With their farms buried, many of the local residents emigrated to Canada. Askja last erupted in 1961. *Map F3*

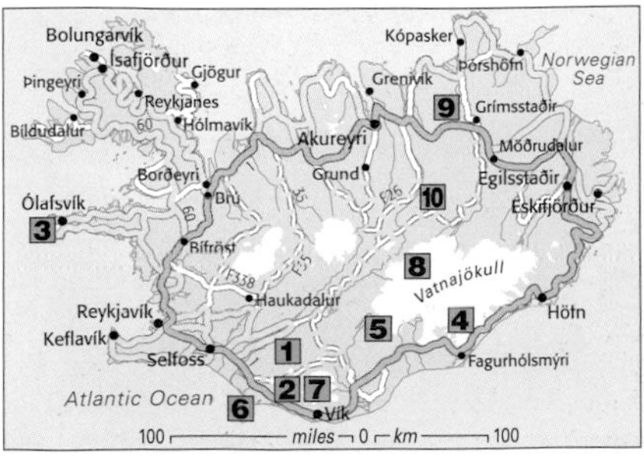

Left **Vox** Right **Fiskmarkaðurinn**

TOP 10 Places for Fine Dining

1 Grillið

This old, elegant, beautifully furnished rooftop restaurant on the eighth floor of the Radisson Hotel offers some of the best food in Reykjavík. Top marks go to their pan-fried plaice with Icelandic cheese and grilled langoustine with locally grown kohlrabi. Enjoy an apéritif – and the cityscape – from the Astra Bar. *Map J3 • Radisson Blu Saga Hótel, Hagatorg, 107 Reykjavík • 525 9960 • Open 6–10pm Tue–Sat • kkkk*

2 Perlan

You can't help but be impressed with Perlan's setting: a revolving restaurant under a glass dome with fantastic vistas over the city. Service is excellent and the food good, if not always as outstanding as the location – the grilled lamb fillet is reliable, as are venison dishes. *Map M6 • Öskjuhlíð, 125 Reykjavík • 562 0200 • Open 6:30pm–10:30pm • kkkk*

3 Gallery

The island's most swanky diner, with a lobby full of fine Icelandic artworks and French-trained chef Friðgeir Eiríksson at the helm. Service is faultless and the menu based on classic French cuisine: go for the fried monkfish and fennel. Extensive but pricey wine list. *Map L3 • Hótel Holt, Bergstaðastræti 37, 101 Reykjavík • 552 5700 • Open noon–2pm, 6:30–10:30pm • kkkk*

4 Vox

Stylish and innovative, this place heads the trend for fresh Icelandic ingredients – seafood straight off the trawlers, game from specialist farms and charr fished locally. Their bistro offers a lunch buffet. *Map R4 • Hilton Reykjavík Nordica, Suðurlandsbraut 2, 108 Reykjavík • 444 5050 • Open 11:30am–10:30pm Wed–Sat, 11:30am–3pm Sun • kkkkk*

5 Grillmarkaðurinn

"The Grill Market" has award-winning chefs who work closely with local organic farmers and producers. As a result, the dishes are always fresh, seasonal and delicious. Try the salted cod with lobster salad, Jerusalem artichokes and apples two ways. *Map L2 • Lækjargata 2A, 101 Reykjavík • 571 7777 • Open 11:30am–2pm Mon–Fri, 6–10:30pm Sun–Thu, 6–11:30pm Fri & Sat • kkkk*

6 Kolabrautin

Enjoy neo-Nordic dishes with a contemporary twist as you look

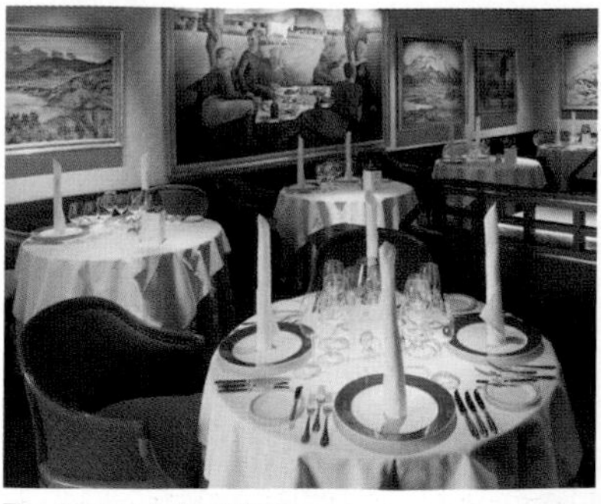

The elegant interior of Gallery

A bottle of fine wine costs the same as a meal for one.

out at one of the best panoramic views of the city from the fourth floor of the Harpa concert hall. The cocktail bar is also one of the finest in Reykjavík *(see p77)*.

7 Kopar
This charming seafront restaurant is the country's first to offer Icelandic rock crab. Sip innovative cocktails like the lime pie mojito, or savour the delectable cod tongues, served with sherry, lemon and garlic cream cheese. *Map K1 • Geirsgötu 3, 101 Reykjavík • 567 2700 • Open 11:30am–2pm Mon–Sat, 6–10:30pm Sun–Thu, 6–11.30pm Fri & Sat • kkkk*

8 Fiskmarkaðurinn
"The Fish Market" is Asian and the sushi outstanding. Like several top-notch restaurants, it sources local produce where possible. The tasting menu, for the whole table, is very good value. *Map K2 • Aðalstræti 12, 101 Reykjavík • 578 8877 • Open 11:30am–2pm, 6–11:30pm daily • kkkkk*

9 Sjávargrillið
For excellent seafood right in the city centre, try this cosy candlelit restaurant, offering traditional specialities such as marinated minke whale, puffin and skyr. *Map L3 • Skólavörðustíg 14, 101 Reykjavík • 571 1100 • Open 11am–4pm Mon–Sat, 5–10pm Mon–Sun • kkkk*

10 Fjöruborðið
Famed for its lobster, this restaurant is located in an old timber building in Stokkseyri, an hour's drive from Reykjavík. The rest of the menu features lamb and other local stalwarts. Book in advance. *Map C5 • Eyrarbraut 3a, Stokkseyri • 483 1550 • Open Jun–Aug: noon–9pm daily; Oct–Apr: 5–9pm Wed–Fri, noon–9pm Sat & Sun; May & Sep: 5–9pm Mon–Fri, noon–9pm Sat & Sun • kkkk*

Top 10 Icelandic Foods

1 Lamb
The mainstay of Icelandic cuisine, lamb is eaten fresh, smoked, turned into sausages, or preserved in whey after pressing.

2 Lobster
Superb and plentiful, best served as tails with butter and, perhaps, a little garlic seasoning or cream.

3 Salmon
Wild-caught Atlantic salmon is firm and rich; usually served smoked or marinated with herbs as butter-soft *graflax*.

4 Caviar
Iceland's supplies come from capelin and lumpfish, not the classic sturgeon, but are just as delicious.

5 Cod
Most often snacked on as dried, chewy *harðifiskur*, but also cooked fresh and used in soups.

6 Hákarl
Greenland shark, fermented in sand for six months to break down toxins. Eye-wateringly strong.

7 Brennivín
Icelandic vodka, flavoured with caraway seeds and affectionately known locally as "Black Death". Use sparingly.

8 Skyr
Like a thick, set yoghurt, available in any supermarket in a range of flavours.

9 Arctic Charr
Freshwater fish with a beautifully subtle flavour. The best come from Þingvallavatn and Mývatn.

10 Ptarmigan
Plump, partridge-like bird which takes the place of turkey in Iceland at traditional Christmas meals.

For a key to price ranges **See p77**.

Left **Icelandic Fish & Chips** Right **Interior of Jómfrúin**

TOP 10 Cheaper Eats in Reykjavík

1 Grænn Kostur

Vegetarians and vegans can choose from a wide range of options at this old restaurant, including dishes that are yeast-, gluten- and sugar-free. Portions are generous and the prices are relatively low. Try their soups and curry dishes, but don't forget to leave room for the delicious desserts. Menu changes daily. *Map L3 • Skólavörðustíg 8b • 552 2028 • Open 11:30am–9pm Mon–Sat, 1–9pm Sun • k*

2 Café Garðurinn

This small vegetarian café has a set menu that changes weekly. Flavour combinations are inventive and delicious. They offer a range of crêpes, flans, stews and pastas, but their forte is tasty soups (served with bread) and quiches. The "dish of the day" plus soup is excellent value. They serve great coffee and cakes too. *Map M2 • Klapparstígur 37 • 561 2345 • Open 11am–6:30pm (to 8:30pm May–Sep) Mon, Tue, Thu & Fri, 11am–5pm Wed, noon–5pm Sat • k*

Laundromat Café

3 Jómfrúin

Calling this place a Danish sandwich shop does not do it justice: a good *smørrebrød* (open sandwich) involves a choice of prawns, herring, smoked lamb, cheese and countless other garnishes served on a thick slice of heavy rye bread, and Jómfrúin delivers in style. Do include the fried plaice in your selection. *Map L2 • Lækjargata 4 • 551 0100 • Open 11am–6pm daily • k*

4 The Tower

As the highest restaurant in Iceland, this place is renowned for its generous weekend brunch buffets – soup, salads, eggs, bacon, steak and chocolate cake. The restaurant is located on the 19th floor of "The Tower", Iceland's tallest building, a glass high-rise in Reykjavík's Kópavogur suburb. *Map Q5 • Smáratorg 3, 201 Kópavogur • 575 7500 • Open 6–11pm Thu–Sun, 11am–3pm Sat & Sun • kkk*

5 Laundromat Café

A laundromat by day (the machines are hidden away), this friendly café serves good breakfasts and great brunches. There's a wide range of books, newspapers and magazines to read, board games to play, and a wonderful playroom and reading lounge for children downstairs. By night the café turns into a lively bar. *Map L2 • Austurstræti 9 • 587 7555 • Open 8am–1am Mon–Thu, 8am–3am Fri, 10am–3am Sat, 10am–1am Sun • kk*

For more restaurants **See pp40–41, 77.**

6 Búllan

Standing isolated on a corner at the harbour entrance inside a 1950s concrete shell, this tiny, glass-fronted diner does just one thing – burgers – and does them extremely well. This is a great place if you need a cheap, decent, filling meal after staggering off a whale-watching boat. Be prepared to queue up as it is always busy. Map K1
• Geirsgata 1 • 511 1888 • Open 11:30am–9pm daily • k

7 Krúa Thai

One of the few places left in Iceland where you can get an economical, real restaurant meal – even if it's only a single course. All the old favourites, from panang curry to *tom kha gai*, are served in a relaxed, fast-food ambience. The beer is not too expensive either. Map L2
• Tryggvagata 14 • 561 0039
• Open 11:30am–9:30pm Mon–Fri, noon–9:30pm Sat, 5–9:30pm Sun • k

8 Icelandic Fish & Chips

Up at Reykjavík's old harbour, this tidy café delivers just what it says: choose from Icelandic cod, plaice, halibut or "catfish" served with a variety of flavoured mayonnaise and oven-grilled chips. Everything is organic, tasty and well cooked. Map K2
• Tryggvagata 8 • 511 1118
• Open 11:30am–9pm Mon–Fri, noon–10pm Sat & Sun • kk

Þrír Frakkar

9 Þrír Frakkar

Set in a warm, pink building in a quiet residential area, the "Three Overcoats" specializes in seafood, with excellent trout, lobster and soups served in a French–Asian fusion. The whale steak, pan-fried guillemot breast, smoked puffin and horse tenderloin are cooked in traditional Icelandic style. Map L3
• Baldursgata 14 • 552 3939 • Open 11:30am–2:30pm, 6–10pm Mon–Fri, 6–11pm Sat & Sun • kkkk

10 Ítalía

An unpretentious Italian restaurant, Ítalía has been around for years and manages to deliver satisfying, enjoyably tasty portions of pasta, pollo and pizza in a good-natured, homey environment. It is hard to single any one dish out, but their parma ham pizza, penne à la arrabiatta and baccalà are a cut above other dishes. Map L2
• Laugavegur 11 • 552 4630 • Open 11:30am–11:30pm daily • kkkk

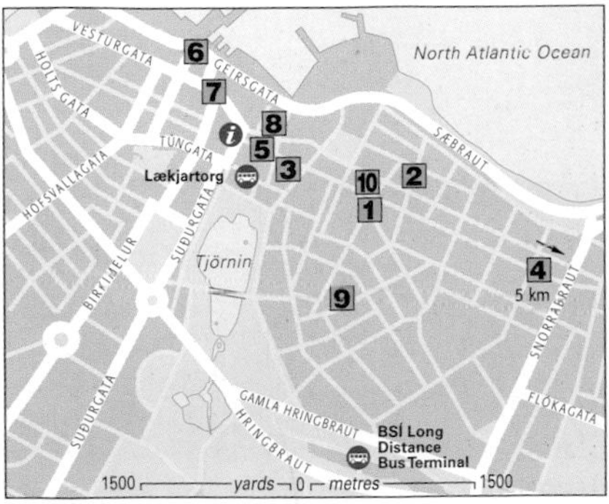

For a key to price ranges **See p77**.

Left **Götubarinn, Reykjavík** Right **Kaffi Amor, Akureyri**

TOP 10 Bars, Clubs and Cafés

1 Austur Steikhús

A trendy but classy steakhouse and bar in the heart of Reykjavík, Austur Steikhús serves steaks that are a fusion of Icelandic beef and Japanese and French cooking. However, the kitchen is open only from 6pm to 10pm – then from Thursday to Saturday, Austur turns into a favourite party venue for local celebrities and media people. *Map L2 • Austurstræti 7, 101 Reykjavík • 568 1907 • Open 11am–10pm Mon–Wed, 11–1am Thu, 11–4:30am Fri, 6pm–4:30am Sat*

2 B5

Another multi-function venue, B5 is a laid-back café by day (with a proper library), which transforms into a popular bar-club after dark. It has two private lounges (one built in an old bank vault) available for hire, if you are planning a party. *Map L2 • Bankastræti 5, 101 Reykjavík • 552 9600 • Open 10:30am–midnight Mon–Wed, 10:30–1am Thu, 10:30–4:30am Fri–Sun*

3 Lebowski Bar

Big Lebowski movie fans will appreciate this quirky bowling-themed bar, its delicious burgers, and 18 variations of the White Russian cocktail. Play "spin the wheel" to get free drinks. DJs and bands play to a packed house on weekends. *Map M2 • Laugavegur 20a, 101 Reykjavík • 552 2300 • Open 11:30–1am Sun–Thu, 11:30–4am Fri & Sat • www.lebowski.is*

4 Micro Bar

Blink and you'll miss this hole in the wall at the back of the City Hotel. Choose from 80-90 different kinds of craft beers, ales, stouts and lagers, including brews you won't find anywhere else in Iceland. It's run by the folks behind the microbrewery, Gæðingur, in the north. *Map L2 • Austurstræti 6, 101 Reykjavík • 847 9084 • Open 2pm–midnight daily*

5 Bjarni Fel

Locals love this sports bar, named after Icelandic football legend and sports commentator, Bjarni Felixson. The multiple screens ensure you won't miss a thing as you enjoy a good selection of pub food and cold beer. *Map L2 • Austurstræti 20, 101 Reykjavík • 561 2240 • Open noon–1am Sun–Thu, noon–4:30am Fri & Sat*

The bar at B5, Reykjavík

Nightclubs do not get going until 11pm.

6 Prikið

A 50s-style diner as well as a nightclub, Prikið offers classics such as milkshakes, American pancakes and chicken burritos. It is a perfect spot for people-watching thanks to its location on the main shopping street. During the day it is a cosy café; at night it transforms into a lively hip-hop hang-out with a packed dance floor *(see p76)*. *Ⓢ Map L2 • Bankastræti 12, 101 Reykjavík • 551 2866 • Open 8–1am Mon–Thu, 8–4:30am Fri, noon–4:30am Sat, noon–1am Sun • www.prikid.is*

7 Kaffibarinn

The distinctive corrugated red iron exterior, just off Reykjavík's main shopping area, conceals Kaffibarinn's dark interior with cable-top candles and arty magazines. It is a trendy and popular place to meet up for the first beer of the evening, and hosts pub bands from time to time. *Ⓢ Map L3 • Bergstaðastræti 1, 101 Reykjavík • 551 1588 • Open 4:30pm–1am Sun–Thu, 3:30pm–4:30am Fri & Sat • www.kaffibarinn.is*

8 Kaffi Amor

Set right on the "circle", Akureyri's downtown square, Kaffi Amor is about the only café outside Reykjavík that can really claim a touch of the city's chic ambiance. It is a great place just to hang out over a coffee during the day, making use of the outdoor seating and just watching the crowds. After dark, come for a beer, occasional live bands or simply to watch major sports events on TV. *Ⓢ Map E2 • Ráðhústorg 9, Akureyri • 461 3030 • Open 11–1am Sun–Thu, 11–4am Fri & Sat*

Lebowski Bar, Reykjavík

9 Slippbarinn

The impressive cocktail menu changes monthly, but the harbour views from this bar remain consistently inspiring. Located in the Icelandair Hotel Reykjavík Marina, Slippbarinn hosts Icelandic music, art and stand-up comedy shows. Brunch is served on weekends and happy hours are from 6 to 8pm everyday. *Ⓢ Map K1 • Mýrargata 2, 101 Reykjavík • 560 8080 • Open 11:30am–midnight Sun–Thu, 11:30–1am Fri & Sat • www.slippbarinn.is*

10 Götubarinn

This charming bar in the centre of Akureyri boasts an excellent selection of beers. Its unique interior design, including old street signs, pays homage to Akureyri's history. A popular choice for a night out in the city. *Ⓢ Map E2 • Hafnarstræti 95-96, 600 Akureyri • 462 4747 • Open 5pm–1am Thu, 5pm–4am Fri & Sat*

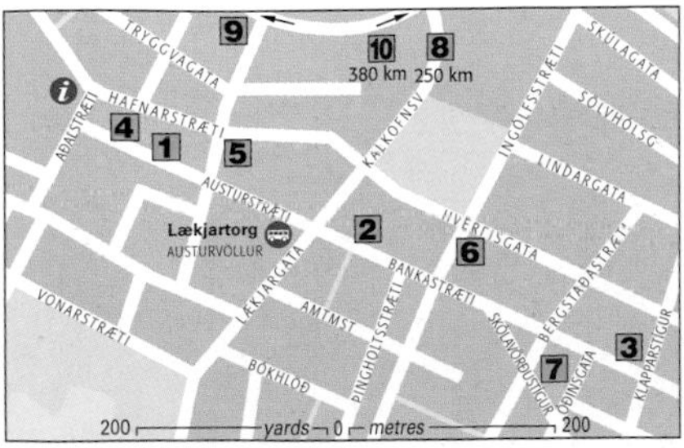

Iceland's legal drinking age is 20.

Left **Feeding ducks, Tjörnin** Centre **Young girl riding a horse** Right **Bæjarins Bestu wagon**

TOP 10 Things to Do With Kids

1 Go Swimming
Swimming pools are great places for children to burn off excess energy, especially after long car journeys. Just about every town in Iceland has a heated pool, making it an easy option. Though most of the pools are outdoors, they are especially fun in winter, when snow is falling.

2 Feed the Birds at Tjörnin
In Reykjavík, pick up a loaf of bread from the nearest bakery and head to Tjörnin *(see p74)* to feed whooper swans, greylag geese, mallards and eider ducks – in June and July there are a lot of cute ducklings around too. Just watch out for pushy seagulls trying to muscle in.

3 Visit the Museums
Iceland's most engaging museums for children are the open-air Árbæjarsafn *(see p61)*; and Brúðuheimar, a museum of puppetry in Borgarnes *(see p63)*; the Saga Centre at Hvolsvöllur, full of swords and dioramas; Borgarnes Settlement Centre, showcasing spooky re-creations of Egil's Saga; and Húsavík Whale Museum, with its skeletons and marine mammal displays.

Swimming pool, Laugardalur

4 Eat a Hot Dog
Not exactly a cultural high point, but eating a *pylsur* (hot dog) from Bæjarins Bestu wagon in central Reykjavík is a rite of passage for young Icelanders, who form long queues outside this unpretentious mobile stand. The reason? The hot dogs taste great – though you might want to hold the onions. *Map L2*
• Tryggvagata, 101 Reykjavík

5 Visit Reykjavík Harbour
Reykjavík has a busy harbour, with all types of colourful fishing boats and trawlers sailing in and out or hauled up on slipways for repairs. Look in the waters and you might also see jellyfish. Snack along nearby Geirsgata at either Búllan café *(see p43)* for burgers, or at Icelandic Fish & Chips *(see p43)* on Tryggvagata. *Map K1*

6 Go Horse Riding
Short and stocky Icelandic horses are even-tempered, making them child-friendly and a good choice for first timers. Most of the riding schools are very flexible with their schedules and duration of rides and cater especially to children *(see p50)*.

Botanical Gardens, Reykjavík

7 Picnic at Reykjavík Botanical Gardens

A pleasant place for a family outing and picnic, just a short way from downtown Reykjavík *(see p73)*. There is plenty of soft grass, ducks and geese wandering about, and – in summer at least – beds of colourful endemic flowers. Don't miss the small zoo, full of native mammals and birds.

8 Enjoy Whale-Watching

There is a good chance of seeing minke and humpback whales, orca, sperm whales and even blue whales as exciting rarities. Húsavík *(see p94)* is the best place for whale-watching.

9 Hunt for Trolls

Trolls, the mean, frightening, mischief-making giants, are said to inhabit several places across Iceland. They turn to stone if caught in the sunlight but their oddly shaped, petrified forms can be seen (if you look hard enough) at many lava fields, mountain outcrops and sea stacks.

10 Go Beachcombing

Icelandic beaches are full of interesting flotsam and jetsam, from bird feathers and tumbled fragments of glass to oddly shaped pebbles, tree trunks (which have floated here from Siberia) and even – if you are really lucky – whale bones.

Top 10 Icelandic Folktales

1 Eyvindur and Halla
Iceland's most famous medieval outlaw, who, along with his wife, Halla, survived 20 years on the run.

2 Viking Treasure at Skógafoss
Legend has it that a Viking named Þrasi hid his hoarded gold under Skógafoss.

3 The Beast of Hvalfjörður
This evil, red-headed whale terrorized Iceland's west coast until it was lured into a trap.

4 Ormurinn, the Lagarfljót Serpent
Iceland's elusive version of the Loch Ness Monster is said to inhabit Lögurinn Lake near Egilsstaðir.

5 Berþór
A friendly giant who lived at Bláfell, near Geysir, and died around 1000.

6 The Lovestruck Shepherd
A favourite tale about a young man who waded across the River Hvítá to propose to a shepherdess.

7 Sæmundur the Wise
Founder of an 11th-century ecclesiastical school, who frequently took on and always defeated the Devil.

8 The Origin of Óxarár Falls
Said to have been created around AD 930 when River Óxará at Þingvellir was diverted.

9 Were-Seals
Seals are thought to sometimes adopt human form, especially ones that swim close to shore.

10 Snorri
The wily thief Snorri escaped pursuit inside a small cave at Þórsmörk – it is near the bus stop.

Left **Hiking in Skaftafell** Right **Golf in Reykjavík**

TOP 10 Outdoor Activities

1 Hiking
Nothing gets you closer to Iceland's raw, natural landscape than hiking across it, following established trails ranging from an hour to a week. The pick of these are at Landmannalaugar, Jökulsárgljúfur, Skaftafell and Þórsmörk, where you can navigate grassy meadows with wildflowers, lava fields, black-sand deserts and icefields. *Hiking organizations: www.fi.is, www.utivist.is, www.mountainguides.is*

2 Swimming
Just about every Icelandic town has an outdoor geothermal swimming pool heated to 28°C (82°F), always with accompanying "hot pot" tubs at 34–38°C (93–100°F), and sometimes with saunas and water slides.

3 Horse Riding
Iceland's specific breed of horses arrived with the Vikings. Though lacking the size and speed of Arab horses, they have a unique gliding gait, called "tölt", used for moving softly over the rough terrain. Many riding schools and farms offer excursions. *www.eldhestar.is, www.ishestar.is*

4 Fishing
Recreational deep-sea angling is in its infancy here and most people fly-fish for trout, salmon or charr *(see pp64–5)*. A permit is essential: those for trout and charr are easy to find on the spot, but for salmon you need to apply in advance. *www.icelandangling.com*

5 River Rafting
What Iceland's rivers lack in size they more than make up for in drama, tearing through narrow volcanic gorges, forming lively rapids. Two of the longest – the Þjórsá and the Hvítá – are accessible for white-water rafting, with trips during the summer. *www.arcticrafting.is, www.rafting.is*

6 Snowmobiling
Snowmobiling or skidooing is an expensive but exhilarating way to tear across snowfields and glaciers at 40 kmph (25 mph). The best place to try it is at Skálafellsjökull, an outrunner of Vatnajökull. *www.glacierjeeps.is*

7 Jeep Touring
The harsh Interior – a spread of rough lava fields, gigantic icecaps and gravel plains braided by glacial rivers – is navigable only by high-clearance 4WDs. Public buses fit the bill and many private operators offer tours in off-road jeeps. *www.glacierjeeps.is*

Jeep crossing a stream in the Highlands

Preceding pages **Kayaking with a glacial backdrop**

8 Skiing and Snowboarding

There are established winter skiing and snowboarding venues around Reykjavík, Akureyri, Hlíðarfjall and in the West Fjords, complete with bunkhouses, ski lifts and graded runs. The most accessible is Bláfjöll, outside Reykjavík and the summer slopes at west Snæfellsjökull, with winter cross-country opportunities around Mývatn. *www.skidasvaedi.is*

Skiing in Arnarstapi

9 Scuba Diving

There is only one area to scuba dive in Iceland – Silfra and other spots around Þingvallavatn. Silfra is rated as one of the best freshwater sites in the world, with crystal-clear, pale blue water and submerged lava formations as the main draws. *Map C5 • www.dive.is, www.diveiceland.com*

10 Golf

Iceland's first golf clubs were founded in the 1930s, since then there has been an explosion of interest in the sport. There are currently over 65 courses, ranging from quirky 9-holers to internationally recognized 18-hole greens. Events include Akureyri's Arctic Open and the Volcano Open in Heimaey island *(see pp36–7)*.

Top 10 Places to Bathe and Swim

1 The Blue Lagoon
Surreal blue water, steam and black lava boulders feature at this ultimate bathing hot spot *(see pp10–11)*.

2 Laugardalur
Reykjavík's best public pool, complete with separate children's play pool and a steam room *(see p73)*.

3 Borgarnes
The town's swimming pool has exceptional views from the water's edge. *Map B4 • Open 7am–9pm Mon–Fri, 9am–6pm Sat & Sun • Adm*

4 Landmannalaugar
Natural hot springs surrounded by lava walls and orange and grey rhyolite mountains *(see pp24–5)*.

5 Jarðböðin
Mývatn's answer to the Blue Lagoon, set up on a hillside among live volcanic scenery *(see p17)*.

6 Selárdalslaug
Tiny public pool near Vopnafjörður, beside the fast-flowing green waters of the Selá river. *Map G2 • Open 10am–10pm daily*

7 Krossneslaug
Unforgettable hot springs and bathing pool in the north, near Norðurfjördur *(see p89)*.

8 Hofsós
Located on the sea shore, the waterline of this pool appears to merge with the ocean. *Map D2*

9 Grettislaug
Remote natural hot tub in the northwest, bathing place of Viking outlaw Grettir *(see p93)*.

10 Laugarvatn
Huge outdoor pool at the National School for Sports near Geysir. *Map C5 • Open 10am–9pm Mon–Fri, 10am–6pm Sat & Sun • Adm*

Left **Eider duck, Vigur** Centre **Exhibit of basalt columns, Viðey** Right **Ptarmigan, Hrísey**

TOP 10 Offshore Islands

1 Viðey
Key historical figures have settled on this flat speck of land just off Reykjavík, amongst them the country's last Catholic bishop, Jón Arason, and sheriff Skúli Magnússon, who built Iceland's first stone house here in 1755. Today it is a stage for the circular Lennon Imagine Peace Tower and the night-time light show. *Map P5 • Daily ferries from Reykjavík • www.videy.com*

2 Lundey
There are plenty of places called Lundey around Iceland – the name means "Puffin Island" – but this is the closest spot to Reykjavík where you can actually see the bird in question, at least while they are nesting between April and August. You cannot land here, but cruises circle Lundey daily in summer. *Map P5 • Cruises from Reykjavík • www.elding.is*

3 Vigur
Out in the West Fjords, this remote, elongated islet makes a great half-day trip from Ísafjörður to see Arctic terns, puffins and especially eider ducks, whose warm, insulating down is commercially gathered for stuffing duvets and jackets. Only discarded chest feathers are collected and the birds are not harmed. *Map B2 • Daily ferry from Ísafjörður mid-Jun–late Aug • www.vesturferdir.is*

4 Hrísey
Up on the north coast near Akureyri, this island is famous for the colossal number of wild, but completely tame, ptarmigans that live here. Though common all over Iceland these birds can be rare in some years, so this is where to come if you have been unable to see them elsewhere. *Map E2 • Daily ferry from Árskógssandur • www.visitakureyri.is*

5 Grímsey
Iceland's northernmost point and the only part actually crossed by the Arctic Circle – meaning the sun really does not set here for a few days either side of 21

Picturesque view of Hrísey

"ey" at the end of a word means "island".

Sleepy island of Flatey

June and does not rise at all in late December. The island's cliffs are full of seabirds. A great day-trip destination. ✎ *Map E1 • Ferry safari from Dalvík Mon–Wed, Fri at 9am; many flights a week from Akureyri • www.akureyri.is/grimsey-en/grimsey-island*

6 Papey

Papey (Monks' Island) is named after the Christian hermits who are believed to have been living here when the Vikings arrived in Iceland. Today the 2 sq km (1 sq mile) island, rising just 60 m (197 ft) out of the sea, is home to thousands of puffins, a few sheep and the smallest church in the country. ✎ *Map H4 • Daily ferry from Djúpivogur Jun–Aug*

7 Flatey

Although hard to believe, this sleepy island halfway across Breiðafjörður between Snæfellsnes and the West Fjords housed an important 12th-century monastery. Later it became famous for the *Flateyjarbók*, an illuminated medieval manuscript featuring the *Greenland Saga*, now kept in Reykjavík's Culture House. The island's east forms a reserve for nesting seabirds. ✎ *Map E2 • Daily ferry from Stykkishólmur–Brjánslækur • www.seatours.is*

8 Heimaey

This 3-km- (2-mile-) long island off the south coast has enough birds, volcanoes, Viking history and walks to occupy you for a couple of sunny days. The town of the same name occupies the north end of the island and is famous for being nearly annihilated during a volcanic eruption in 1973. ✎ *Map C6 • Daily ferry Herjólfur from Þorlákshöfn or Landeyjahöfn mid-May–mid-Sep; flights from Reykjavík and Bakki • www.eimskip.is*

9 Eldey

About 15 km (9 miles) off Iceland's southwesternmost tip, Eldey's distinctive, rocky, sheer-sided cliffs rise 77 m (250 ft) straight out of the Atlantic. The top forms a level platform, home to Europe's largest gannet colony. Sadly, this is also where the last known pair of great auks were killed in 1844. ✎ *Map B5*

10 Surtsey

Surtsey dramatically popped out of the waves during an underwater volcanic eruption southwest of Heimaey in 1963. Following erosion over the years, the island's size is now around 1.5 km (1 mile) across. Scientists are studying Surtsey to see how plants and animals colonize new lands. A special UNESCO reserve, this island is off-limits. ✎ *Map C6*

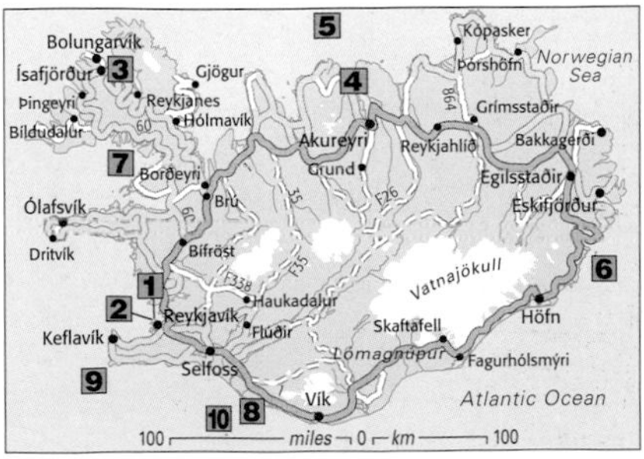

People playing accordions at the Culture Night in Reykjavík

TOP 10 Festivals

1 Menningarnótt

One night in mid-August is designated Culture Night and downtown Reykjavík is closed to traffic as stages are set up, performers throng the streets and fireworks explode over the city. The entertainment is mainly amateur but well-known groups also participate at times.

2 Kvikmyndahátið

A selection of the year's best in World Cinema gets a screening at the Icelandic Film Festival in late September, with events all around town. Look out for retrospectives of Icelandic masterpieces such as *Djöflaeyjan (Devil's Island), 101 Reykjavík* and *Sódóma Reykjavík* – the last a definite cult classic. *www.riff.is*

3 Reykjavík Arts Festival

This two-week showcase of concerts, operas, dances and theatre has been held every mid-May since 1970. Drawing local and international talent, it is organized at various venues, including the National Gallery, Nordic House and Harpa *(see p72)*, with spin-off events around Iceland throughout the summer. *www.listahatid.is*

4 Djasshátíð – Reykjavík Jazz Festival

The latest in jazz and blues comes to Reykjavík for the last two weeks of August. There is always a smattering of international stars but the surprise is the quality and abundance of local talent. Do not miss the "Guitar Party" event. *www.reykjavikjazz.is*

5 Fiskidagurinn Mikli

Early August sees Dalvík, the non-descript fishing village near Akureyri, draw the crowds with its "Fish Soup Day", a sort of eccentric, friendly social event that Iceland should be famous for. Apart from outdoor seafood buffets, look for homes displaying flaming torches – a sign that free fish soup is available. *Map E2*
• *www.fiskidagur.muna.is*

6 Myrkir Músíkdagar

Held in February during odd-numbered years, the "Dark Music Days" festival brightens up Reykjavík's winter gloom with workshops and almost exclusively Icelandic contemporary music performances ranging from avant garde to opera.
www.myrkir.is

Giant puppet at Reykjavík Arts Festival

Gay Pride festival, Reykjavík

7 Gay Pride

Held annually since 1999, Reykjavík's Gay Pride festival goes from strength to strength, though the August timetable is asking a bit from the weather and rain is not unknown during the Saturday parade, which starts at Hlemmur bus station and winds through the downtown. *www.reykjavikpride.com*

8 Þjóðhátíð Vestmannaeyjar

Westman Island Festival is not for the faint-hearted: camping for 4 days in August in a sodden volcano crater, serenaded by an unending line-up of Icelandic rock at maximum decibels and getting drunk enough to try skinny-dipping in the sea along with thousands of others. *www.dalurinn.is*

9 Kirkjubæjarklaustur Chamber Music Festival

This festival, held on the first weekend in August, showcases international talent among south Iceland's largest lava fields. It also provides a chance to explore small-town Iceland. *Map E5* • *www.kammertonleikar.is*

10 Síldarævintýri

Every August the small north coast town of Siglufjörður, once the North Atlantic's busiest herring port, holds a music festival known as the Herring Adventure in honour of the fish. It includes everything from traditional folk singers to Sigur Rós. *Map D2*

Top 10 Icelandic Musicians

1 Björk

This singer is Iceland's best-known musical export, though nowhere near as popular at home as abroad.

2 Sigur Rós

"Post-rock" band, Sigur Rós is a crossover between pop, classical and folk music and has absolutely unique vocals.

3 KK

Folk guitarist Kristján Kristjánsson is Iceland's Arlo Guthrie, quite often teaming up with veteran Magnús Eiríksson

4 Stefán Íslandi

Born in 1907, Stefán Íslandi performed as an opera tenor in the US until his death in 1994.

5 Sigrún Hjálmtýsdóttir

A leading opera soprano and jazz singer, Sigrún Hjálmtýsdóttir has performed with José Carreras and Placido Domingo.

6 Kristinn Sigmundsson

Massive operatic bass, Sigmundsson is well suited to playing Mephistopheles in Berlioz' *Faust*.

7 Mugison

Iceland's version of fusion-delta blues, this slide guitarist from West Fjords, Mugison, has an astounding voice.

8 Emiliana Torrini

Part Icelandic, part Italian, sweet-voiced singer Torrini is the first Icelander to top the German music charts.

9 Bubbi Morthens

Morthens is a mix of punk, Bruce Springsteen and Johnny Cash – minus the hair.

10 Kristinn Árnason

Brilliant classical guitarist, Árnason effortlessly manages the crossover into rock.

Left **A campsite** Centre **Svartifoss signage** Right **Eyjafjallajökull icecap**

Top 10 Hiking Trails

1 Laugavegur

This stunning 4-day hike runs from Landmannalaugar, past hot springs and obsidian massifs, to the snowbound Hrafntinnusker Plateau, descending steeply to the green valley around Álftvatn. After many glacial rivers, a grey gravel desert at the foot of the Mýrdalsjökull icecap and canyons along Markarfljót, the trail ends in Þórsmörk's woodland *(see p25)*.

2 Fimmvörðuháls

An overnight trek from Skógar to Þórsmörk can be done separately or as an extension to Laugavegur. From Skógar, climb the steps to the top of the waterfall and follow the river upstream to cross the pass between Eyjafjallajökull *(see p38)* and Mýrdalsjökull icecaps, descending to Þórsmörk. *Map D6 • Summer buses to Skógar and Þórsmörk • Trail: open mid-Jun–Sep; www.fi.is*

3 Esja

Esja's 914-m- (2,999-ft-) high plateau rises unmistakably above the bay north of Reykjavík. Its snow-streaked slopes appear to mutate with the changing light – the colours shift from deep brown to pale blue. A return hike from the Mógilsá forestry station takes about four hours. *Map Q5*

4 Þingvellir

Þingvellir's mossy valley floor is criss-crossed by easy hiking trails of 1- to 3-hour durations. Stick to marked paths, as vegetated lava flows conceal deep fissures. There are good views along the valley beside abandoned farm buildings at Skógarkot. *Map C5 • Daily buses from Reykjavík*

One of the Þingvellir trails

5 Svartifoss

Skaftafell National Park's most beautiful feature, Svartifoss (Black Falls), is located on an easy hiking trail atop Skaftafell Plateau. From the car park near Bölti guesthouse follow signposts for 10 minutes to the falls that drop into a 30-m (98-ft) gully *(see pp18–19)*.

6 Ásbyrgi

The top of this huge, curved cliff-face makes an excellent vantage point for admiring the north of Jökulsárgljúfur National Park. From the park headquarters, follow footpaths for 5 km (3 miles) through woodland to the top of Ásbyrgi *(see pp18–19)*.

Always carry food and water when hiking in Iceland.

7 Heiðmörk Park

A 28 sq km (11 sq mile) spread of lava, woodlands and picnic sites on the edge of Reykjavík city, with easy walking paths looping through it. Extend an excursion here by making a 3-hour circuit of the adjacent lake Elliðavatn, to view a variety of Iceland's flora. *Map Q6*

8 Hveragerði

The steamy hills and valleys immediately north of Hveragerði make for a good half-day hike from town, with hot springs along the way – bring a towel. There is a pegged path but be prepared for boggy ground, a couple of river crossings and unpredictable boiling vents. *Map C5*

9 Arnarstapi to Hellnar

The short coastal walk between the two small villages offers great seascapes and views of Snæfellsjökull's white cone. On the way look out for the statue of Bárður Snæfellsás and nesting Arctic terns. *Map A4*

10 Þórsmörk

This beautiful highland valley, with a braided glacial river, is overlooked by Mýrdalsjökull. Carry a map, as few of the many day trails are marked. *Map D6 • Daily buses from Reykjavík • Only accessible mid-Jun–Aug • www.thorsmork.is*

View of Mýrdalsjökull

Top 10 Icelandic Wildflowers

1 Mountain Avens (Holtasóley)
Iceland's national flower, whose small fleshy leaves and yellow-centred white petals stand about 7 cm (3 in) high.

2 Arctic River Beauty (Eyrarós)
Late-flowering plant with distinctive symmetrical, pointed red petals and long leaves.

3 Moss Campion (Lambagras)
Spongy clumps of this bright pink flower brighten up the muddy, shaley slopes.

4 Wild Pansy (Þrenningarfjóla)
Beautiful little plant with violet and yellow petals, common locally and abundant in June.

5 Bladder Campion (Holurt)
White flower found in small spreads, with a lilac-pink sack behind the petals.

6 Wild Thyme (Blóðberg)
Tiny, ground-hugging plant with deep red or purple flowers and distinct thyme smell.

7 Wood Cranesbill (Blágresi)
Widespread plant with geranium-like leaves and purple, five-petal flowers; favours woodland edges and reaches 30 cm (12 in) or more.

8 Butterwort (Lyfjagras)
Small, solitary plant with hanging blue flowers and cross-shaped leaves at ground level.

9 Northern Green Orchid (Friggjargras)
Easily overlooked in the grass, but look for pointed leaves and little white flowers.

10 Purple Saxifrage (Vetrarblóm)
Widespread but very early-flowering, ground-hugging plant with little pink blooms.

Left **Steam vent at Námaskarð** Right **The Blue Lagoon**

TOP 10 Hot Springs and Geysers

1 Geysir

Now just a flooded crater at the top of a mound, Geysir once set the benchmark for erupting hot spouts worldwide until its subterranean vents became clogged with debris. A big earthquake in 2008 might have cleared some of them: new bubbling and hissing are the first signs of action for decades *(see pp12–13)*.

2 Jarðböðin Nature Baths

This mineral-rich natural spa uses its dramatic location on a steaming volcanic ridge overlooking Lake Mývatn to good effect. Take a look across the road too, where people have dug pits in the hot soil, covered them with metal lids, and use them as ovens for baking bread – and cooking sheep heads *(see p17)*.

Jarðböðin nature baths

3 The Blue Lagoon

Only Icelanders could turn the outflow from a geothermal power station into the country's premier tourist attraction. At the Blue Lagoon they have done a superb job, even if the first thing you see is people emerging from the milky-blue water with their faces covered in the fine white silt which is also sold as a beauty product *(see pp10–11)*.

4 Deildartunguhver

Water emerging at 97°C (207°F) at Deildartunguhver, Europe's largest hot spring, fills the skies with steam near the historic hamlet of Reykholt in west Iceland. There's no bathing pool here – the water is pumped straight to the coastal towns of Borgarnes and Akranes – but the violently spluttering vent is impressive. *Map C4*

5 Landmannalaugar

Popular with Icelanders and tourists alike, Landmannalaugar is the country's finest natural bathing pool – you just can't beat the feeling of soaking away in the hot stream here as a wall of lava towers overhead and fractured orange mountains frame the distance. No other part of the Interior is so wild, yet so accessible *(see pp24–5)*.

6 Strokkur

Geysir's stand-in, Strokkur *(see pp12–13)* is far more reliable too, erupting 10 times in an

Left **Strokkur** Right **Hveravellir**

hour – even at its peak, Geysir often lay quiet for days at a time. Strokkur is the largest continually active geyser in Iceland (and the one featured in most photographs), reaching impressive heights on a good day.

7 Seltún

Down on the Reykjanes Peninsula near Reykjavík, there was a decent geyser at Seltún in Krýsuvík, until the entire spring exploded in 1999, leaving behind a grey, bubbling pool. But smaller hot springs still seep out of the hills above, making for an interesting half-hour walk – do not leave the marked paths. *Map B5*

8 Námaskarð

This hillside east of Lake Mývatn, dotted with roaring steam vents and coloured mud pools, does a great job of demonstrating how raw and powerful nature can be *(see p17)*. The setting, with a lonely, sulphur-rich orange plain stretching away to the south, only adds to the impression.

9 Hveravellir

Famous hot spring on the interior Kjölur Route, it was once used by the 17th-century outlaw Eyvindur for warmth and to cook stolen sheep. A great spot to pause during the rough, 5-hour ride from Gullfoss to Akureyri and enjoy a soak in the cooler spa pool alongside. *Map D4*
• Summer buses from Reykjavík and Akureyri • Bus schedules: www.bsi.is

10 Hengill

Popular hiking area west of Hveragerði with hot springs and steam vents. Many of them are being diverted for geothermal energy projects – power plants and miles of silver coloured pipes for Reykjavík's water and electricity are visible nearby. *Map B6*

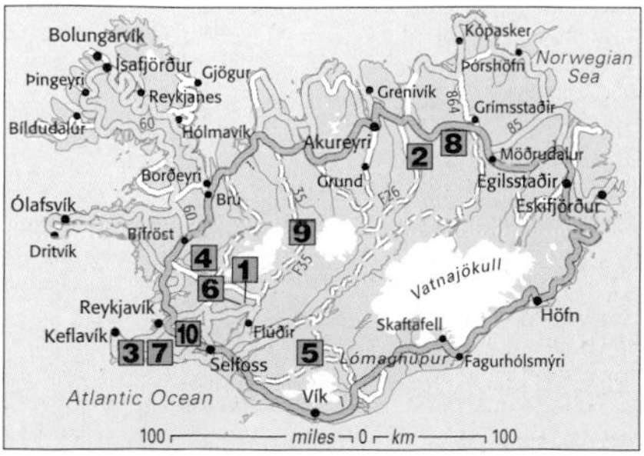

Left **Settlement Exhibition** Centre **Reykjavík Art Museum** Right **Ásmundur Sveinsson Museum**

TOP 10 Museums in Reykjavík

1 Listasafn Íslands (National Gallery)

A core collection of works by seminal Icelandic artists such as Ásgrímur Jónsson contrasts with avant-garde installations by the likes of Hrafnkell Sigurðsson and Krístján Guðmundsson. The gallery showcases regular archaeological and historical exhibitions. It is one of the main venues for the annual Reykjavík Arts Festival in June *(see p71)*.

2 Þjóðminjasafn Íslands (National Museum)

An absorbing exploration of Iceland's history and culture begins with evidence of the earliest visitors (Roman coins found along the south coast), Viking graves, carved doors, medieval church sculptures and 19th-century clothing, and winds up with contemporary pop music and genetic research into the national family tree *(see p72)*.

National Museum

3 Reykjavík Art Museum

At the waterfront branch of the museum's three sites, the main focus is on the artist Erró, born in Iceland in 1932. Of the sculptures, paintings and drawings on display, the most striking are his multi-coloured collages of mythical heroes. Another branch focuses on the work of Jóhannes Kjarval *(see p72)* and the third, on Ásmundur Sveinsson *(see opposite)*. *Map L2 • Hafnarhús, Tryggvagata 17 • 590 1200 • Open 10am–5pm Mon–Sun, 10am–8pm Thu • Adm (under-18s free) • www.artmuseum.is*

4 Landnámssýningin (Settlement Exhibition)

The centrepiece to this excellent subterranean museum is the oval foundation wall of a Viking long-house, with a distinctive under-lying layer of volcanic ash, dated AD 871. Holographic dioramas and artifacts, including wooden farm implements and corroded axes, bring it all to life. Look for sacrificial cow bones among the foundations *(see p71)*.

5 Einar Jónsson Sculpture Museum

Einar Jónsson's monumental pieces owe a good deal to the early 20th-century nationalist movements across Europe, with heroic marble figures in dramatic, iconic arrangements. One of the favourites is St George resting on the crucifix of his sword, holding his shield aloft, with the dragon coiling behind *(see p74)*.

Many museums are closed on Mondays.

Sigurjón Ólafsson Sculpture Museum

6 Sigurjón Ólafsson Sculpture Museum

Located along the foreshore, this gallery was founded by the artist's widow. It displays Sigurjón's modernist, abstract works in timber, stone and metal, ranging from smoothly contoured sculptures to giant installations looking like totem poles made out of scrap iron and driftwood *(see p74)*.

7 Gerðarsafn

This gallery concentrates on modern and contemporary artists with an eclectic range of styles and tastes and features a collection of work by Gerður Helgadóttir (1928–1975). Check the website for current exhibitions. *Map Q5 • Hamraborg 4, 200 Kópavogur • 570 0440 • Buses from Lækjatorg or Hlemmur to Hamraborg • Open 11am–5pm Tue–Sun • www.gerdarsafn.is*

8 Víkin – Reykjavík Maritime Museum

The museum at Reykjavík's old harbour tries to convey a flavour of life on the ocean. Pick of the exhibits is the magnificent Ódinn, a coastguard vessel docked at the museum's pier. *Map K1 • Grandagarður 8, 101 Reykjavík • 517 9400 • Open Jun–mid-Sep: 10am–5pm daily; mid-Sep–May: 11am–5pm Tue–Sun; closed Dec & Jan • Adm • www.sjominjasafn.is*

9 Árbæjarsafn

A former farm has been converted into an open-air museum of old buildings, farm machinery and period artifacts. The best permanent exhibit is the turf-roofed timber house from the late 19th century. Regular events, when the machinery is fired up and domestic animals wander around, bring the place to life. *Map P6 • Kistuhyl 4, Árbær • 411 6300 • Bus 12, 19 or 24 from Hlemmur & Lækjartorg • Open Jun–Aug: 10am–5pm daily; Sep–May: 1–2pm Mon, Wed, Fri or by appointment • Adm • www.minjasafnreykjavikur.is*

10 Ásmundur Sveinsson Sculpture Museum

Part of the Reykjavík Art Museum, this building is an attraction in itself, but the real pleasure is walking around the sculpture garden outside, full of Ásmundur's powerful depiction of themes from history and folklore, influenced by cubism and African tribal art. Inside are smaller pieces in a variety of media *(see p74)*.

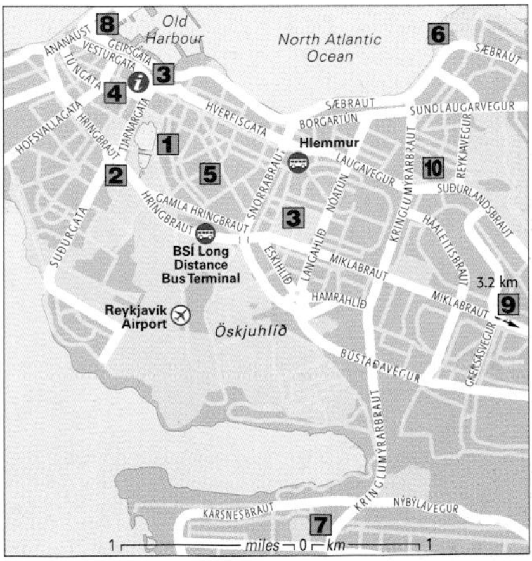

Left **Herring Era Museum** Right **A display at the Icelandic Emigration Centre**

Top 10 Museums Around Iceland

1 Borgarnes Settlement Centre

The museum is in two halves and its entry price includes audio guides. Upstairs, Iceland's settlement is covered in detail, from a pneumatic longship prow to impressions of how the islands looked then with more trees and no sheep. Downstairs, *Egil's Saga* is brought to life with depictions of key scenes from this violent tale *(see p79)*.

Settlement Centre

2 Icelandic Emigration Centre

The museum's lonely setting on the north coast gives some idea of the feelings endured by the thousands of 19th-century Icelanders who left for Canada following a catastrophic series of harsh winters and volcanic eruptions. *Map D2 • Hofsós • 453 7935 • Buses in summer • Open Jun–Aug: 11am–6pm daily • Adm • www.hofsos.is*

3 Skógar Museum

The museum's collection documents over 1,000 years of life. There is a brass ring off a Viking treasure chest, traditional turf buildings, a Bible from 1584 (Iceland's first printed book), a fishing boat and clothing. *Map D6 • Skógar • 487 8845 • Buses from Reykjavík and Höfn • Open May & Sep: 10am–5pm; Jun–Aug: 9am–6pm; Oct–Apr: 11am–4pm daily • Adm • www.skogasafn.is*

4 Herring Era Museum

A sleepy place today, Siglufjörður was – until fish stocks declined during the 1960s – the busiest herring port in the country, its harbour crammed with boats. The museum documents those hectic times in photos, models and dioramas, including photographs of the armies of "herring girls" who cleaned and salted the catches. *Map D2 • Snorragata 15, Siglufjörður • 467 1604 • Buses in summer • Open Jun–Aug: 10am–6pm; Sep–May: 1–5pm daily • Adm • www.sild.is*

5 Orkusýn Geothermal Energy Exhibition

The state-of-the-art exhibition shows how geothermal energy is used in Iceland and its potential as a non-polluting energy source. The guided tour is excellent and the interactive multimedia exhibits are fascinating too, especially the Seismic Simulator – though not for the faint-hearted.

Skógar Museum

Ⓢ *Map C5 • Hellisheiði Power Plant, 20 mins drive from Reykjavík towards Hveragerdi on Route 1 • Open 9am–5pm daily • Adm • www.orkusyn.is*

6 Húsavík Whale Museum

Overlooking Húsavík harbour, where whaling boats are now used for whale-watching tours, this museum uses videos, relics and whole minke and humpback skeletons to provide information on whales. It is essential viewing before heading seawards to see them. Ⓢ *Map E2 • Hafnarstétt 1, Húsavík • 414 2800 • Open Apr, May & Sep: 9am–4pm daily; Jun–Aug: 8am–6.30pm daily; Oct–Mar: 10am–3:30pm Mon–Fri • Adm • www.whalemuseum.is*

7 Brúðuheimar Centre for Puppet Arts

This is both a museum of puppetry and a puppet theatre. Exhibits are displayed in lovingly created theatrical settings. Workshops teach the ancient art of puppetry, from mysterious shadow puppets to stringed marionettes, and visitors can watch the process of crafting a puppet. Ⓢ *Map B4 • Skúlagata 17, Borgarnes • 530 5000 • Open 10am–10pm daily in summer • Adm • www.bruduheimar.is*

8 Langabúð

The oldest wooden building on Djúpivogur harbour, Langabúð was built as a warehouse in 1790 and is now a cultural centre, folk museum and a memorial to the local artist Ríkarður Jónsson (1888–1977). He taught drawing and sculpture and his works are on display here. It also has a coffee shop. Ⓢ *Map G4 • Djúpivogur • 478 8220 • Buses run between Höfn and Egilsstaðir in the summer • Open Jun–Sep: 10am–6pm daily • Adm*

Exhibit at the Húsavík Whale Museum

9 Turnhús

Ísafjörður was settled in the 1580s and later became a busy port for saltfish. The town has a museum located in the 18th-century Turnhús (the towerhouse was a lookout post) which documents those times. Photographs show that the town centre has changed little since the early 20th century. Ⓢ *Map B2 • Turnhús, Suðurgata, Ísafjörður • 896 3291 • Open 15 May–15 Sep: 9am–6pm • Adm • www.nedsti.is*

10 Viking World

The modern, glass-sided museum just outside Keflavík houses the *Íslendingur*, a full-scale reproduction of a wooden Viking longship unearthed in Norway in the 1880s. *Íslendingur* was built by captain Gunnar Marel Eggertsson, who sailed in it to New York in 2000 to celebrate the millennium of the Viking discovery of North America. Ⓢ *Map B5 • Víkingabraut 1, 260, Reykjanesbær • 422 2000 • Open summer: 11am–6pm; winter: noon–5pm daily • Adm • www.vikingaheimar.com*

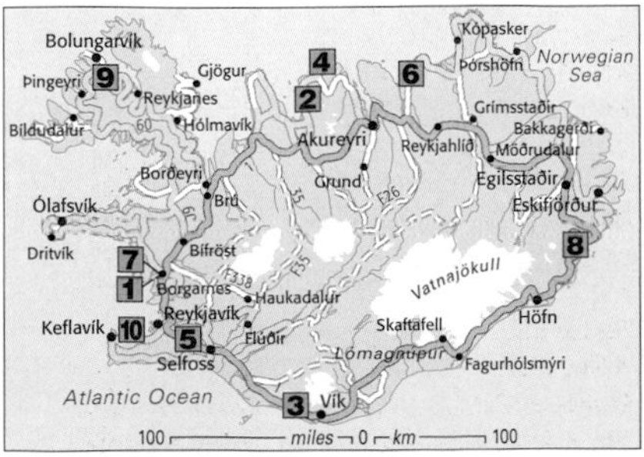

Left **Brown trout** Right **Norðurá**

TOP 10 Fishing Spots

1 Elliðaár
Despite a hydro power dam, each year around 1,500 salmon are hauled out of this 10-km- (6-mile-) long river, which runs right through Reykjavík's suburbs. This is the country's only salmon river offering half-day permits, making it slightly more affordable than most. *Map P5 • 568 6050 • www.icelandicrivers.com*

2 Laxá í Kjós
About an hour's drive from Reykjavík, this 25-km- (16-mile-) long river comprises waterfall pools, rapids and long, flat, stretches – in short, perfect conditions for salmon. Lodge owners offer permits, guides and 4WDs. *Map Q6 • 577 2230 • www.hreggnasi.is*

3 Laxá í Aðaldal
Misleadingly known for its salmon fishing – *laxá* means "salmon river" – this is a classic brown trout river, flowing 60 km (37 miles) north from Lake Mývatn to the sea through some gorgeous scenery. Over 4,000 fish, weighing up to 5 kg (10 lb), are caught here each year. *Map E2 • 557 6100 • veidi@laxamyvatn.is*

4 Hítará
The 30 km- (19-mile-) long river has an annual bag of 350 salmon, a few trout and charr. It is popular due to its accessible, wild location and an eccentric, old lodge nearby. Book in advance. *Map B4 • 568 6050 • www.icelandicrivers.com*

5 Vatnasvæði Lýsu
A series of interconnected lakes and streams on the Snæfellsnes Peninsula, and one of the few single locations in the country where you have a good chance of catching trout, charr and salmon. It is unreliable, so less expensive. *Map B4 • 557 6100*

6 Norðurá
This is an expensive, prestigous salmon river with fickle water levels and an annual catch upwards of 1,500 fish. Although the Norðurá is 65 km (40 mile) long, only 12 people can fish here at a time. There is a lodge in the area for a stay and meals. *Map C3 • 568 6050 • www.icelandicrivers.com*

7 Vatnsdalsá
One of north Iceland's better salmon rivers with about 20 km (12 miles) of suitable terrain along its 40-km (25-mile) length, made famous by British author

Angling at Hítará

For more on fishing permits **See pp123, 126.**

and one-time owner John Ashley-Cooper. The annual haul of 1,000 fish is not huge, but they tend to weigh above average. Salmon over 5 kg (10 lb) are released back for spawning numbers.
Map D3 • 551 2112 or 897 1498

8 Elliðavatn

This lake just southeast of Reykjavík is the source of the Elliðaár river, with a nature reserve on the eastern side and a riding track along the shore. Look out for the brown trout.
Map Q6 • For permits: 568 6050

Fishing for trout

9 Hópið

An estuary lake spread over 30 sq km (19 sq miles), it is best known for charr and trout, which are netted by locals through the spring and autumn; anglers get sole access from mid-June until mid-August. *Map C3 • 466 4000, 898 4006 • www.veidikortid.is*

10 Ytri-Rangá

Near Hella in south Iceland, this is the richest salmon river in the country thanks to a smolt release programme – a staggering 14,315 were landed in 2008, with an average weight of over 4 kg (8 lb). You need to plan the trip in advance. *Map C5 • 557 6100 • www.fishpal.com/Norse/Iceland*

Top 10 Icelandic Fish

1 Cod
The backbone of Iceland's traditional fishing industry, the cod used to appear on the Icelandic coat of arms.

2 Haddock
A popular deepwater fish around 1-m (3-ft) long, with big spawning grounds in the southwestern Icelandic waters.

3 Halibut
Huge, bottom-dwelling flatfish weighing up to 200 kg (440 lb), with both eyes on the same side of its body.

4 Ocean Perch
Large-eyed deepwater fish with bright red scales; tastes excellent when grilled whole.

5 Ocean Catfish
Abundantly fanged and with sweet, firm flesh, the ocean catfish is also known as the wolf fish. It is unrelated to the fresh-water catfish.

6 Atlantic Salmon
Freshly caught Atlantic salmon is some of the best in the world and tastes even better smoked.

7 Brown Trout
Excellent sport and eating fish, the brown trout is mainly confined to freshwater rivers and lakes in Iceland.

8 Arctic Charr
Another fine fish for eating, it is often hooked in winter by fishing through holes in the frozen lakes.

9 Monkfish
Ghastly looking, globular, flattened sea fish with a huge semi-circular mouth and sweet, delicious meat.

10 Lobster
Also known as the langoustine or Norway lobster, it is another favourite on Reykjavík's restaurant menus.

Trout and charr permits are not as expensive as salmon permits.

Left **Detail of Þingeyrarkirkja** Centre **Viðimýri's turf chapel** Right **Church at Grund**

TOP 10 Churches

1 Dómkirkjan

This small, stone and corrugated-iron Lutheran cathedral was built between 1788 and 1796 just as Reykjavík, previously just a collection of farm buildings and warehouses, began to coalesce into Iceland's first town. The interior shows off the building's unadorned but beautiful and simple proportions to best effect. *Map L2 • Austurvöllur Square, Reykjavík • 520 9700 • Open 10am–4:30pm Mon–Fri*

2 Landakotskirkja

Iceland's Catholic faith was fiercely stomped out in 1550, so it is not surprising that this cathedral dates back to only 1929. Perhaps not to offend Protestant feelings, the building is functional and plain in the extreme, and it is only the font at the entrance and statue of the Virgin Mary that gives the denomination away. *Map K2 • Túngata 15, Reykjavík • 552 5388 • Open 7:30am–6:30pm daily • www.catholica.is*

3 Skálholtskirkja

Iceland's first bishopric, from 1056 until 1801, Skálholt became an important educational centre and, at one point, was the country's largest settlement. The memorial outside is dedicated to Iceland's last Catholic bishop, Jón Arason, and the 13th-century tomb is that of bishop Páll Jónsson. Concerts are also held at the cathedral. *Map C5 • Skálholt, Biskupstungur • 486 8870 • Daily bus from Selfoss, mid-May–Sep; tours from Reykjavík • www.skalholt.is*

4 Hóladómkirkja

Seat of Iceland's second bishopric since the 12th century, this remote cathedral dates to the 1760s, though some sculptures – and the ornate altarpieces – are centuries older. The country's first printing press was founded here by bishop Jón Arason in 1530, who is buried in a small adjacent chapel. *Map D2 • Hólar í Hjaltadal • 895 9850 • Open Jun–Sep: 10am–6pm daily (regular buses) • www.kirkjan.is/holadomkirkja*

Plain exterior of Landakotskirkja, Reykjavík

5 Bænahús at Núpsstaður

Wedged below tall cliffs, Núpsstaður is a collection of antique turf farm buildings, including Bænahús church, which was once considered Iceland's remotest holding despite its proximity to the coast.

Until the 1850s the nearest harbours were at distant Eyrarbakki and Djúpivogur, and stock had to be transported inland via the daunting highland roads. *Map E5 • Núpsstaður, near Kirkjubæjarklaustur*

Inside Hallgrímskirkja, Reykjavík

6 Hallgrímskirkja

Vast in scale as it stands proudly over Reykjavík, Hallgrímskirkja is not a cathedral, though it is Iceland's biggest church. Designed in 1945, construction was undertaken by a family firm of just two people and the building work dragged on, incredibly, until 1986 *(see p72)*.

7 Þingeyrarkirkja

This beautiful stone church up in northern Iceland stands close to a Viking assembly site and the presumed location of the country's first monastery. Þingeyrarkirkja's medieval alabaster altar was carved in England. The ceiling of the church is painted blue and studded with hundreds of gold stars that create a gorgeous effect *(see p96)*.

8 Víðimýri

The 19th-century tiny turf chapel at Víðimýri is one of only six surviving in Iceland, with a attractive timber interior. Check out the walls, weatherproofed by stacking thick slices of earth in a "herring bone" pattern, and the pretty summertime flowers growing on the grassy roof. *Map D3 • Víðimýri, Skagafjörður • 453 6173 • Open Jun–Aug: 9am–6pm daily • Adm*

9 Strandakirkja

Standing beyond a seashore hamlet at the eastern end of the Reykjanes Peninsula, Strandakirkja is a picture-perfect 19th-century church, painted pale blue and built on a firm base of square-cut lava blocks. According to legend, it was funded by grateful sailors who made it ashore at this very spot during a storm. *Map C5 • Selvogur, near Þorlákshöfn • 483 3771 • Open May–Sep*

10 Grund

Most unusually for Iceland, this church has an onion-domed cupola topping its wooden tower and Romanesque mini-spires. Though the building is fairly recent – built by trader Magnús Sigurðsson in 1905 – Grund was once a wealthy holding. The treasures of the church include a 15th-century chalice, kept at the National Museum in Reykjavík. The church is privately owned, but visitors are welcome. *Map E3 • Grund, Eyjarfjörður*

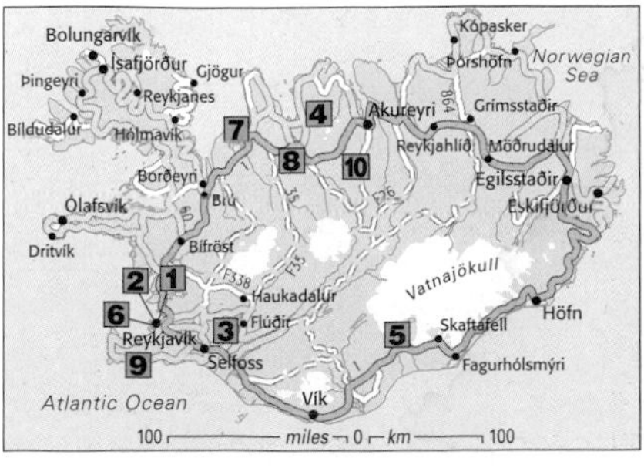

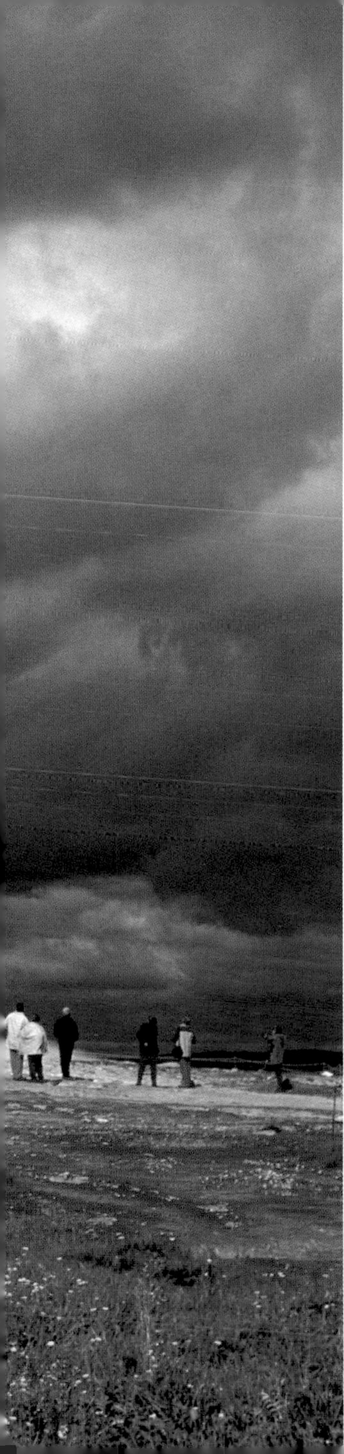

AROUND ICELAND

Left **Laugardalur swimming pool** Right **Botanical Gardens**

Reykjavík

REYKJAVÍK CAPITAL AREA COVERS THE CITY CENTRE, *plus a handful of satellite suburbs. The city's tiny core focuses on a historic precinct of lanes near the old harbour, easily covered on foot in a day. While the municipal buildings are made of stone or concrete – practical protection against the fierce winter winds – most of the area is residential, comprising old wooden houses, weatherproofed in brightly coloured corrugated iron. Here you will find most of the shops, cafés, restaurants and famously raucous nightclubs, alongside museums and galleries. A distinctive landmark is Öskjuhlið hill, with a scattering of more distant sights and modern suburbs.*

Harpa building

TOP 10 Sights

1. Historic Midtown and Harbour
2. Landnámssýningin
3. Þjóðmenningarhúsið
4. Listasafn Íslands
5. Þjóðminjasafn Íslands
6. Hallgrímskirkja
7. Kjarvalsstaðir (Reykjavík Art Museum)
8. Harpa
9. Perlan
10. Laugardalur Park and Recreation Area

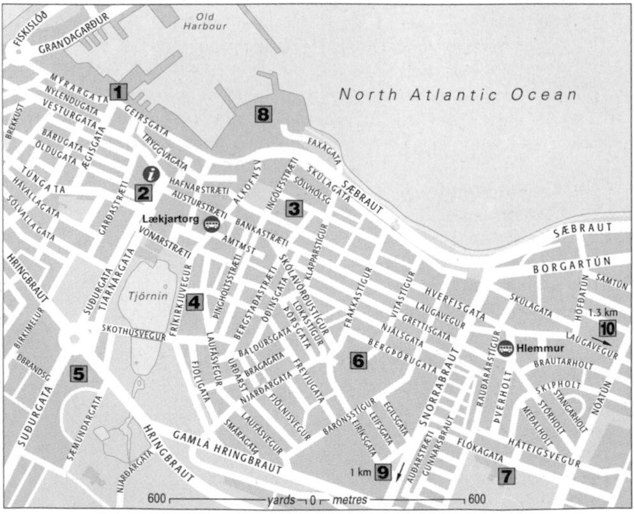

Preceding pages **Strokkur geysir**

Buildings in the historic midtown area

1 Historic Midtown and Harbour

Reykjavík's historic midtown occupies the site of Iceland's first Viking settlement (now being excavated near Austurvöllur Square) and the city's oldest standing building (an 18th-century wooden storehouse on the adjacent Lækjatorg Square). Off Austurvöllur, a statue of Jón Sigurðsson *(see p31)* faces the 1881 Parliament Building, which replaced the Alþing's original home at Þingvellir. Just north, check out the busy old harbour and the whaling fleet. *Map K1*

2 Landnámssýningin (Settlement Exhibition)

This impressive exhibition comprises the in-situ remains of a large Viking-age longhouse, possibly belonging to Iceland's first official settler, Norwegian Ingólfur Arnarson, who sailed to Iceland around AD 870. A visit here will surround you in a factual past; there are virtually no other contemporary remains in such good condition. Its location under the capital's streets makes it even more incredible. *Map K2 • Aðalstræti 16 • 411 6370 • Open 10am–5pm daily • Adm • www.reykjavik871.is*

3 Þjóðmenningarhúsið (Culture House)

Stored in Denmark for centuries, Iceland's precious medieval manuscripts were returned to the country in the 1970s and are now displayed in the old National Library. Look for the *Codex Regius* containing the "Edda", the main source for Norse mythology; the *Flateyjarbók*, which includes the only known copy of the *Greenland Saga*, documenting Leifur Eiríksson's discovery of "Vínland" (North America); and the huge compendium of sagas known as the *Möðruvallabók*. There is also an excellent account of the composition and history of the manuscripts. *Map L2 • Hverfisgata 15 • 545 1400 • Open 11am–5pm daily • Adm (Wed free) • On-site café (weekends); guided tours available • www.thjodmenning.is*

4 Listasafn Íslands (National Gallery)

The nation's main collection of art is housed in a former warehouse where blocks of ice, cut from the nearby lake, were once stored. The gallery concentrates on early 20th-century Icelandic painters. There is a continual rotation of the estimated 10,000 works and regular space is dedicated to contemporary and traditional art, so there should be something of interest even if you have visited before. *Map L3 • Fríkirkjuvegur 7 • 515 9600 • Open 10am–5pm; closed Mon • www.listasafn.is*

Viking era manuscripts, Culture House

The Settlement of Reykjavík

When Ingólfur Arnarson first saw Iceland on his voyage from Norway in AD 870, he threw overboard his valuable wooden seat-posts and vowed to settle wherever they washed up. They were finally found in a broad, fertile, steamy inlet on the island's southwest, which Ingólfur named Reykjavík ("Smoky Bay").

5 Þjóðminjasafn Íslands (National Museum)

This museum documents Iceland's history and culture from the earliest evidence of settlement to the present. A floor is devoted to the early period – DNA testing is used to trace Viking heritage. Whether it is Viking grave goods, medieval statues or Björk's musical career, the chances are you will find something interesting over the two floors. *Map K3 • Suðurgata 41 • 530 2200 • Open 1 May–15 Sep: 10am–5pm daily; 16 Sep–30 Apr: 11am–5pm Tue–Sun • Adm • www.thjodminjasafn.is*

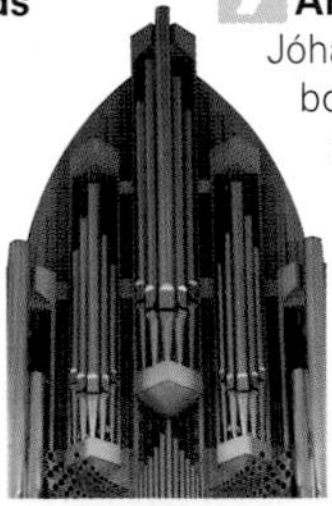

Hallgrímskirkja's organ

6 Hallgrímskirkja

The largest in Iceland, this 73-m- (240-ft-) high church took 40 years to build and resembles a volcanic formation, covered in hexagonal pillars. The interior is unadorned but hearing the organ is an experience; it is a stunning instrument with 5,000 pipes. Take the lift to the tower for views over Reykjavík's colourful rooftops and Leifur Eiríksson's statue. *Map M3 • Skólavörðuholti • 510 1000 • Open 9am–5pm daily • Cathedral free; tower adm • www.hallgrimskirkja.is*

7 Kjarvalsstaðir (Reykjavík Art Museum)

Jóhannes Kjarval (1885–1972), born in a tiny village in the northeast, studied painting in Europe. On returning to Iceland he began incorporating the landscapes into his brightly coloured paintings. Though considered Iceland's greatest artist, his work often controversially blended folklore, Christianity and paganism. Apart from his works, this museum also exhibits contemporary Icelandic as well as foreign art. *Map N4 • Flókagata 24 • 517 1290 • Open 10am–5pm daily • Guided tours by arrangement • www.listasafnreykjavikur.is • Adm*

8 Harpa

Harpa – the Reykjavík Concert Hall and Conference Centre – is the most important classical and performance venue in the country, home to the Iceland Symphony Orchestra and the Icelandic Opera. With a façade by renowned artist Olafur Eliasson, it is a symbol of the revitalization of Reykjavík's historic waterfront and of Iceland's renewed dynamism. *Map L2 • Austurstraeti 17 • 528 5000 • Guided tours in summer • www.harpa.is*

Exhibition at the National Museum

9 Perlan

Just south of the city centre is Perlan ("the Pearl") the mirrored-glass dome atop Öskjuhlið hill. This imaginative building, with six cylindrical water tanks converted into a tourist attraction, has great views and a renowned restaurant *(see p40)*. One tank is the Saga Museum, which brings alive the Viking period with wax dioramas. *Map M6 • Öskjuhlið • Bus 18 from Hlemmur • Saga Museum: 511 1517; open Apr–Sep: 10am–6pm daily; Oct–Mar: noon–5pm weekends; adm; audio guides; www.sagamuseum.is • Building entry free*

10 Laugardalur Park and Recreation Area

East of the centre, Laugardalur Park is a great spot to join local families relaxing. The Botanical Gardens also have a zoo full of native species and a duck pond. You can skate in winters at the adjacent sports centre or visit year-round the naturally-heated 50-m- (164-ft-) long outdoor pool, with three smaller play pools and hot tubs. *Map R4 • Laugardalur • Bus 14 from Hlemmur • Pool: 411 5100; open Apr–Aug: 6:30am–10pm Mon–Fri, 8am–10pm Sat & Sun • Park free; activities adm*

Perlan's entrance

A Day in Reykjavík

Morning

Kick off the day the way many Icelanders do – by having a swim at central **Sundhöllin** indoor pool before work. After a coffee at **Kaffitár** on Bankastræti, head for the **National Museum** and get a solid grounding in Icelandic history, though don't burn out by trying to cover it all on a single trip. Amble down to get some fresh air and feed the birds at **Tjörnin** *(see p74)*, before ducking inside **City Hall** for a look at their giant relief map or to catch a lunch-time concert. Sit out on the grass at **Austurvöllur Square** *(see p71)*, to admire the humble Reykjavík Cathedral, Art Deco Hótel Borg and Parliament House. Then spend half an hour among Viking remains at the excellent **Settlement Exhibition** *(see p71)* located nearby.

Afternoon

Reboot your energy levels with a leisurely bowl of Icelandic lamb soup at **Café Paris** *(see p76)*, then shop for jewellery, clothes or souvenirs along **Laugavegur**. Head uphill, past a street of colourful houses on Klapparstígur, to take in the cityscape from the top of **Hallsgrímskirkja**. If you have room for another museum, soak up some Saga-Age ambience at the **Culture House** *(see p71)*. Walk north to **Harpa** to take in a concert, or to see the striking **Solar Voyager** sculpture and historic **Höfði House** *(see p74)*. Plan an assault of the city's nightclubs – ***Prikið*** *(see p45)*, in the city centre, is the place to start.

Left **Höfði House** Right **View of Viðey island across Stóra tjörn lake**

Top 10 Best of the Rest

1 Noræna húsið

The Modernist Nordic House, designed by Finnish architect Alvar Aalto, hosts exhibitions and concerts. Its library is devoted to Nordic culture. *Map K4 • Sturlugata 5 • 551 7030 • Open noon–5pm Tue–Sun • www.nordice.is*

2 Höfði House

In this simple, whitewashed house, the presidents of Russia and the US, Mikhail Gorbachev and Ronald Reagan, ended the Cold War in 1986. The nearby *Solar Voyager* sculpture honours Viking travels. *Map P2 • Borgatún*

3 Alþingishúsið

This 19th-century rectangular building houses the world's oldest National Parliament, which was founded at Þingvellir in AD 930 and relocated here in 1881. *Map L2 • Austurvöllur • 563 0500 • Open 8am–7pm Mon–Fri • www.althingi.is*

4 Tjörnin

Locals bring their children to feed the ducks, geese and swans at this stone-edged pond in the city centre. *Map K3*

5 Sigurjón Ólafsson Sculpture Museum

Once the studio of artist Sigurjón Ólafsson (1908–1982), this Nordic style seafront building displays his sculptures. Concerts are held here in summer. *Map Q1 • Laugarnestangi 70 • Buses 12 & 15 • 553 2906 • Open Feb–May, Sep–Nov: 2–5pm Sat & Sun; Jun–Aug: 2–5pm Tue–Sun • www.lso.is*

6 Ásmundur Sveinsson Sculpture Museum

With Mediterranean and African influence, this building is as interesting as the displayed works of the renowned sculptor. *Map Q4 • Sigtun • 590 1200 • Open May–Sep: 10am–5pm; Oct–Apr: 1–5pm daily • Adm*

7 Hafnarfjörður

Reykjavík's seaside suburb is home to good restaurants and an annual Viking festival. *Map P6 • Bus 1 from Hamraborg • www.hafnarfjordur.is, www.fjorukrain.is*

8 Viðey

Just off Reykjavík, this grassy isle boasts Iceland's oldest stone building (now a restaurant), thousands of seabirds and the Lennon Imagine Peace Tower. *Map P5 • 15 May–30 Sep: 8 ferries daily from Skarfabakka, and 1 daily from Reykjavík's Old Harbour • www.videy.com*

9 Einar Jónsson Sculpture Museum

Iceland's first modern sculptor, Einar Jónsson's (1874–1954) 300 marble statues are displayed here against vivid backdrops. *Map M3 • Eiríksgata • 561 3797 • Open Jun–15 Sep: 2–5pm Tue–Sun; 16 Sep–30 Nov, 1 Feb–31 May: 2–5pm Sat & Sun • Adm • www.lej.is*

10 Öskjuhlíð

Perlan *(see p73)* is the biggest draw of this wooded hillside, but walking tracks also lead to a sandy bathing beach and a thermal pool nearby. *Map M6*

Most museums offer student and pensioner discounts.

Left **Fríða Frænka** Right **Display at Búrið/The Icelandic Pantry**

TOP 10 Places to Shop

1 Kirsuberjatréð

This unique store, run by a women's cooperative, offers distinctly Icelandic garments, fish-skin accessories, glassware, jewellery and gift items. *Map L2 • Vesturgata 4 • 562 8990 • www.kirs.is*

2 Fríða Frænka

Search for unusual gifts in the old corrugated iron house, stuffed with antique furniture and quirky knick knacks. *Map L2 • Vesturgata 3 • 551 4730*

3 Thorvaldsens Bazar

In business for over a century, this charity shop specializes in handmade jumpers, local woodcarvings, clothing and silver jewellery. *Map L2 • Austurstræti 4 • 551 3509 • www.thorvaldsens.is*

4 Eymundsson

Excellent bookshop with a big range of maps – from road atlases to detailed hiking ones – English books on Iceland, stationery and T-shirts. It has a good café, too. *Map L3 • Skólavörðustíg 11 • 540 2350*

5 12 Tónar

Music CDs and vinyl, with an eclectic inventory of local artists covering jazz, classical and pop. *Map L3 • Skólavörðustíg 15 • 511 5656*

6 Kraum

Local designers display and sell their clothes and accessories here. Look for attractive silver and black lava jewellery. *Map L2 • Aðalstræti 10 • 517 7797 • www.kraum.is*

7 Aurum

Gudbjorg Kristin Ingvarsdottir's jewellery is modelled on Iceland's landscape and flora, using precious metals to create delicate, fluid designs that are both modern and timeless. *Map L2 • Banakstræti 4 • 551 2770 • www.aurum.is*

8 Frank Úlfar Michelsen

Great old-style watchmaker, with a workshop full of half-repaired pre-digital timepieces. Sells Rolexes and other classic wrist watches. *Map L2 • Laugavegur 15 • 511 1900*

9 Búrið/The Icelandic Pantry

Gourmet cheese shop with a tempting selection and local specialities such as birch syrup and rhubarb caramels. Book ahead for a fun Icelandic cheese class and lunch. *Map P3 • Nóatún 17 • 551 8400 • http://blog.burid.is*

10 Kolaportið Flea Market

Join locals and spend a couple of hours sifting through acres of household junk here and you might uncover unexpectedly stylish designer clothing. Good home-grown veggies, too. *Map L2 • Tryggvagata 19 • 562 5030 • Open 11am–5pm Sat & Sun.*

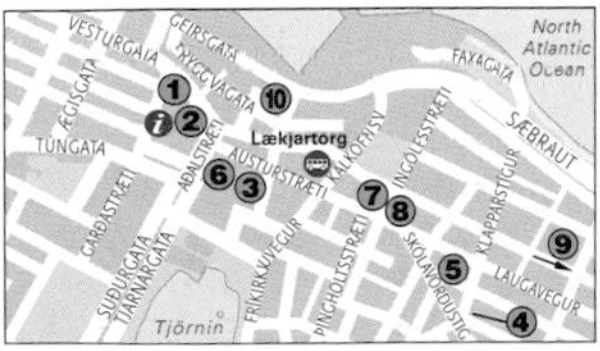

Left **Hornið** Right **Café Paris**

TOP 10 Bars, Cafés and Pubs

1 Café Paris

Try the sandwiches or crêpes for lunch at this café, popular with locals and tourists. Sit outside in good weather. *Map L2 • Austurstræti 14 • 551 1020 • Open 8–2am Fri & Sat, 8–1am Sun–Thu*

2 Prikið

This friendly café-diner, frequented by an arty crowd, has a bar feel by night. There are hip-hop DJs at weekends *(see p45)*. *Map L2 • Bankastræti 12 • 551 2866*

3 Vegamót

A restaurant-bar with a great patio, Vegamót is busy at lunchtime and after office hours. People-watch over a drink, or sample the Mediterranean menu. *Map L3 • Vegamótstigur 4 • 511 3040*

4 Íslenski Barinn

Traditional Icelandic delicacies and beer are served here. There are waffles and coffee every Sunday and live music on Thursday, Friday and Saturday. *Map L2 • Pósthússtræti 9 • 578 2020*

5 Grái Kötturinn

Huge breakfasts are served at this trendy basement café. It's a popular place to get coffee after a night out. *Map L2 • Hverfisgata 16a • 551 1544 • Open 7am–3pm Mon–Fri, 8am–2pm Sat & Sun*

6 Hornið

In business since 1979, this family-run, cosy Italian pizzeria is rumoured to have served the country's first espressos. Their fresh seafood pastas are superb. *Map L2 • Hafnarstræti 15 • 551 3340*

7 Café Rosenberg

A classic folk, jazz and blues bar, this venue serves simple meals too. It has been open for decades, although the original building burned down in 2007. *Map M3 • Klapparstígur 25 • 551 2442*

8 Celtic Cross

Crowds pile in for the exceptional vibe at this popular Irish bar. Sometimes two bands play at the same time. *Map L2 • Hverfisgata 26 • 571 1033*

9 Sandholt

Tasty breads, Danish pastries, quiches, chocolates, sandwiches and superb coffee are served at this family bakery. *Map M3 • Laugavegur 36 • 551 3524*

10 Mokka

Said to be Reykjavík's oldest café (opened in 1958), the no-frills Mokka spearheaded the caffeine culture. *Map L3 • Skólavörðustíg 3a • 552 1174*

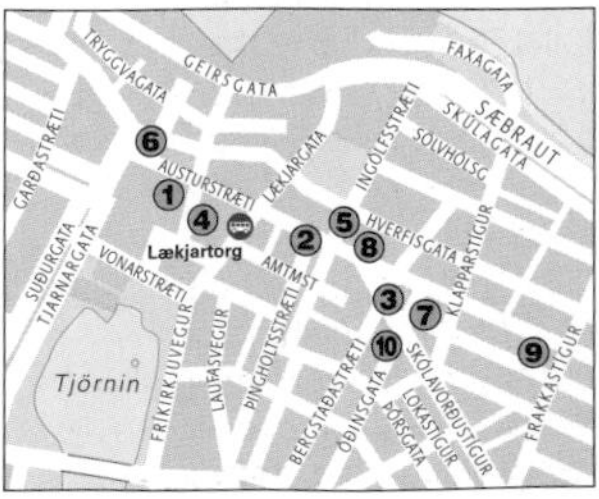

Set menus have to be ordered by the whole table.

Price Categories

For a three course meal for one (without alcohol), with taxes and extra charges.	**k**	under ISK3,000
	kk	ISK3,000–5,000
	kkk	ISK5,000–7,000
	kkkk	ISK7,000–9,000
	kkkkk	over ISK9,000

Left **Fjalakötturinn**

TOP 10 Restaurants

1 Við Tjörnina
At this smart restaurant overlooking Tjörnin, with house speciality seafood dishes, guests can even get a free bag of bread to feed the ducks. *Map L3 • Templarasundi 3 • 551 8666 • kkkk*

2 Kolabrautin
Enjoy Neo-Nordic dishes and innovative cocktails with the best panoramic view of Reykjavík *(see pp40–1). Map L2 • Austurbakki 1 • 519 9700 • Open 11:30am–2pm Mon–Fri, 5:30–10pm Mon–Sun • kkkk*

3 Lækjarbrekka
Housed in an old storehouse in the city centre, this famous eatery is full of period furnishings. It serves top-notch traditional seafood. *Map L2 • Bankastræti 2 • 551 4430 • Open 11am–11pm daily • kkkkk*

4 Humarhúsið
This restaurant, in a 19th-century building, is one of the best places for fresh lobster. Try their "four-course mystery menu". *Map L2 • Amtmannstíg 1 • 561 3303 • kkkk*

5 Caruso
Period furnishings and an Italian menu make this an elegant but not a formal place to dine – they even serve pizzas. There is a bar on the second floor. *Map L2 • Þingholtstræti 1 • 562 7335 • kkkk*

6 Fjalakötturinn
The finest home-grown lamb and salmon compete for your approval with the decor and service. A Viking longhouse was excavated here. *Map K2 • Hótel Reykjavík, Aðalstræti 16 • 514 6060 • kkkk*

7 Einar Ben
It has a limited menu (fish, beef or lamb), but you will probably have the best meal in Iceland at this restaurant. *Map K2 • Veltusundi 1 • 511 5090 • kkkkk*

8 Restaurant Reykjavík
Known for its seafood, this beautiful old wooden warehouse overlooks Ingólfstorg. Try the delicious Portuguese-style cod or visit the adjacent Ice Bar. *Map K2 • Vesturgata 2 • 552 3030 • kkkk*

9 Brauðbær
Enjoy tasty steaks, burgers, club sandwiches and cold *smorrabrauð* dishes here. A kids' menu is available. *Map L3 • Hótel Oðinsvé, Þórsgata 1 • 552 0490 • kkkk*

10 O-Sushi
For raw seafood, try this slick sushi restaurant done in greys, steel and pine. Dishes are colour-coded according to price. *Map L2 • Lækjargata 2a • 561 0562 • k*

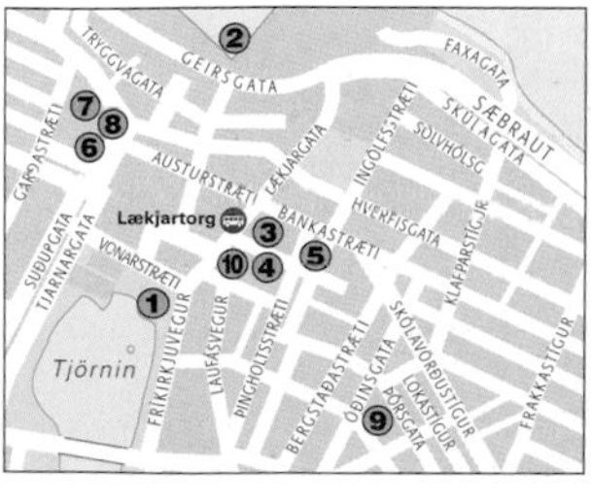

➔ *Autumn is the best time for fresh lamb in Iceland.*

Left **Wild horses, Hvalfjörður** Right **Búðir Hotel, Snæfellsnes Peninsula**

West Iceland and the Snæfellsnes Peninsula

HEADING NORTH FROM REYKJAVÍK, *the highway follows the weather-beaten western coastline, famous for its stormy weather and good farmland. Beyond Hvalfjörður and the exceptional Glymur falls, Akranes reveals itself as a workaday town and, apart from a good museum, there's more cause to pause around atmospheric Borgarnes, once home to the notorious Viking Egill Skallagrímsson. The 13th-century historian, Snorri Sturluson, lived (and was murdered) just inland at Reykholt, close to an attractive set of waterfalls and more saga lore around Laxárdalur. Northwest of Borgarnes, the long Snæfellsnes Peninsula's coastline is dotted with tiny fishing villages and its tip graced by Snæfellsjökull, the conical icecap covering a dormant volcano.*

Cultural Centre, Reykholt

TOP 10 Sights

1. **Borgarnes Settlement Centre**
2. **Reykholt**
3. **Hraunfossar, Barnafoss and Kaldidalur**
4. **Stykkishólmur**
5. **Breiðafjörður and Flatey**
6. **Búðir**
7. **Snæfellsjökull National Park**
8. **Laxárdalur**
9. **Akranes**
10. **Hvalfjörður**

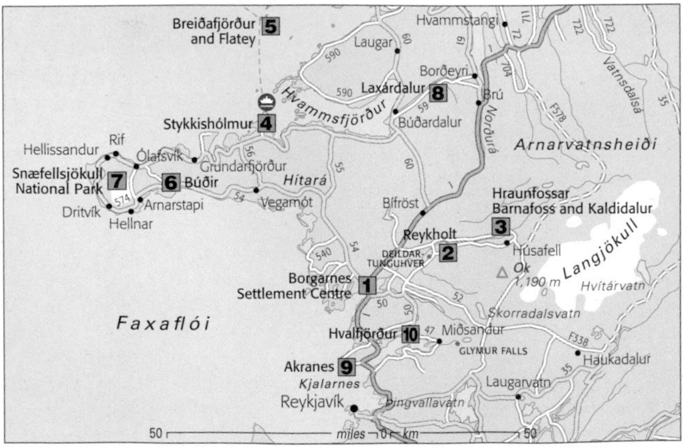

1 Borgarnes Settlement Centre

Iceland's Settlement Period, the Landnám, began in AD 870 when the Viking settlers arrived and lasted until all free land had been occupied around AD 930. This museum explores the period, using archaeological finds and near-contemporary records of the first colonists. A section of the museum celebrates the life of the warrior-poet Egill Skallagrímsson, who was born in Borgarnes.

Map B4 • Brákarbraut 13-15, Borgarnes • 437 1600 • Daily buses from Reykjavík • Open Jun–Aug: 10am–7pm daily; Sep–May: 11am–5pm daily; restaurant: 11am–9pm daily • Adm • www.landnam.is

2 Reykholt

Set in the Reykholtsdalur Valley, the tiny hamlet of Reykholt belies its importance as the home of Snorri Sturluson (1179–1241), the historian who became tangled in Norway's bid to annex Iceland. Snorri was murdered by a rival who had the support of the Norwegian king, Hákon. He was trapped as he fled down a tunnel beneath his farmhouse. His tale is told at Snorrastofa, below Reykholt's church; his thermal bathing pool and restored remains of the tunnel are nearby. *Map C4 • Snorrastofa, Reykholt • 433 8000*

Scene from Egil's Saga, Settlement Centre

• Open May–Aug: 10am–6pm daily; Sep–Apr: 10am–5pm Mon–Fri • Adm • www.snorrastofa.is

3 Hraunfossar, Barnafoss and Kaldidalur

About 15 km (9 miles) east up the valley from Reykholt along Route 518, contrasting twin waterfalls at Hraunfossar and Barnafoss – one a gentle cascade, the other a violent tumble – are worth a stop on the way to Kaldidalur, a stark valley between the icy peaks of Ok and Þórisjökull. The 70-km (44-mile) road, which follows routes 551, 550 and 52 to Þingvellir, is unsealed, though open in summer to ordinary vehicles driven with care (check conditions at www.vegagerdin.is), providing an easy taste of the interior. *Map C4*

4 Stykkishólmur

This pleasant town has old wooden buildings recalling its 19th-century heyday as a herring port. Best of these is the Norska húsið, the Norwegian House. The surrounding countryside is dotted with sites from the *Eyrbyggja Saga* *(see p82)*. Enjoy views of the town from the Library of Water, whose 24 glass columns are filled with water from Iceland's major glaciers. *Map B3 • 438 1640 • Norska húsið: open 1 Jun–31 Aug: noon–5pm daily; www.stykkisholmur.is • Library of Water: open Jun–Aug: 1–6pm daily; May & Sep: weekends; www.libraryofwater.is*

Harbour at Stykkishólmur, Snæfellsnes Peninsula

Egil's Saga

An interesting mixture of history, folklore and political allegory, *Egil's Saga* recounts the roller-coaster life of Egill Skallagrímsson (AD 910–990), a bully of a Viking who spent his youth fighting the Norwegians and his old age fighting everyone else, but was nonetheless a magnificent poet. A must-read, along with *Njál's Saga* and *Laxdæla Saga.*

Church at Búðir

5 Breiðafjörður and Flatey

Breiðafjörður – the huge, wide bay separating the Snæfellsnes Peninsula from the West Fjords to the north – is thick with islands and rocky reefs, providing an ideal breeding ground for marine birds. From Stykkishólmur, you can explore the bay on a tour with Sæferðir (www.seatours.is), or go to Brjánslækur in the West Fjords via Breiðafjörður's largest island, Flatey, once home to an important monastery. For a taste of island life and bird-watching, stay at Flatey's tiny village (www.hotelflatey.is). ⓢ *Map B3*

6 Búðir

Búðir is a minute place on Snæfellsnes' south coast, with just a church and a hotel. One can enjoy beautiful seascapes and views of Snæfellsjökull from here. The dark wooden church dates from 1703, its graveyard and boundaries encroached upon by the Búðahraun lavafield, said to be inhabited by creatures from local folklore. Despite its remote location, the romantic Hótel Búðir *(see p130)* is famous for being a favourite with Nobel Prize-winning author Halldór Laxness. Don't miss the amazing black-sand beach. ⓢ *Map A4*

7 Snæfellsjökull National Park

Based around an ice-capped volcano, this national park featured in the classic tale *Journey to the Centre of the Earth*. It extends over rough, vegetated lava fields to a coastline rich in birdlife. Hiking, skiing or exploration of local villages are all possibilities, and you can easily circuit the park by car in a day *(see pp20–21).*

View of Snæfellsnes Peninsula

8 Laxárdalur

This pretty valley along Route 59 is the setting for the *Laxdæla Saga*, Icelandic literature's great tragic love story. It tells of the beautiful Guðrún Ósvífursdóttir and her four husbands: the first she divorces but the rest perish due to witchcraft, feuding and drowning while she becomes a nun. Only place-names from that time survive, namely the church at Hjarðarholt, and farmsteads at Goddastaðir and Höskuldsstaðir. *Map C3*

9 Akranes

Akranes, Iceland's oldest fishing port, is a good place to experience a down-to-earth, gritty Icelandic town. Fishing is still the main industry and the harbour and processing factory survive alongside the less romantic National Cement Works. The town is famous for its sports club, Íþróttabandalag Akraness, whose football team has won the national games 18 times. The engaging Museum Centre *(see p82)* provides a good reason to visit, though it is a 10-km (6-mile) detour off the highway. *Map B5*

Fishing boat in Akranes Museum Centre

10 Hvalfjörður

Most people use the tunnel under the bay to bypass the 30-km- (19-mile-) deep Hvalfjörður, but miss some classic scenery, including Glymur *(see p32)*, the isle's highest waterfall. Hvalfjörður means "whale fjord", after the number of whales once seen here. It was also a US naval base during World War II and the red barracks have now been turned into holiday homes. *Map C4*

A Day in the West

Morning

Head north from Reykjavík around windswept Kjalarnes, where the road is pinched between the sea and the domineering Esja Plateau. Avoid the 5-km- (3-mile-) long cross-fjord tunnel and follow Route 47 around **Hvalfjörður**. At the head of the fjord, take the 4-km (3-mile) gravel road inland to where the magnificent **Glymur** waterfall cascades down the 200-m- (656-ft-) high cliffs. Continue around Hvalfjörður to rejoin Route 1 and continue to **Borgarnes**. Spend an hour at the **Settlement Centre** *(see p79)*, delving into the lives of Iceland's Viking pioneers. Don't miss out on the spooky dioramas downstairs, retelling the tale of Egil's Saga. Have a quick lunch at the good-value café here.

Afternoon

Make **Deildartunguhver**, Europe's largest thermal spring *(see p58)*, the first stop of the afternoon followed by a further historical halt at **Reykholt**, taking in the Heimskringla Museum, the church and old geothermal bathing pool. From here, follow Route 518 to **Hraunfossar and Barnafoss** *(see pp32–3)*, the latter the setting for a tragic tale of two children who drowned in the rapids here while trying to cross over a lava bridge. Both falls are small but very attractive, especially for keen photographers. At this point you can retrace your route or – though this is an adventurous, summer-only option – follow gravel tracks south via **Kaldidalur** to **Þingvellir** *(see pp8–9)* and head back to Reykjavík.

Left **Old fishing boat outside the Akranes Museum Centre** Right **Cave opening, Surtshellir**

TOP 10 Best of the Rest

1 Borg á Mýrum
Site of Egill Skallagrímsson's home, but nothing contemporary survives. The statue, *Sonatorrek* (Lament for my Dead Sons), is named after his poem. *Map B4*

2 Eiríksstaðir
The reconstructed longhouse of Viking Eirík Þorvaldsson, known as Eirik the Red, and his son Leifur, who explored Greenland and North America. *Map C3 • Eiríksstaðir, Haukadal, 371 Búðardalur • 434 1118 • Open Jun–Sep: 9am–6pm daily • Adm • www.eiriksstadir.is*

3 Gamla Pakkhúsið
This warehouse, built in 1844, houses a café and a folk museum. Photographs and fishing memorabilia outline the town's history. *Map A3 • Ólafsbraut, Ólafsvík • 433 6930 • Open Jun–Aug: 1–6pm daily • Adm*

4 Kerlingarfjall
Route 56 to Stykkishólmur crosses Kerlingarfjall, a mountain said to be haunted by the ghost of a female troll, who turned to stone on her way back from a fishing expedition. *Map B3*

5 Húsafell
Picturesque spread of woodland and meadows east of Reykholt, with an old church, open-air geothermal swimming pool and petrol station serving the scattered community of summer houses used by holidaymakers. *Map C4*

6 Surtshellir
Large subterranean cave near Húsafell, named after giant Surtur. Later used by outlaws, who also hid stolen livestock here. *Map C4*

7 Akranes Museum Centre
Four museums in one centre – Folk, Mineral, Sports and Land Survey Museums. *Map B5 • Að Görðum, Akranes • 431 5566 • Open Jun–Aug: 10am–5pm; Sep–May: 1–5pm daily • Adm • www.museum.is*

8 Berserkjahraun
The *Eyrbyggja Saga* tells how a berserker was promised a local man's daughter if he cleared a path through this lava field, but was murdered once he completed the task. *Map B3*

9 Stykkishólmur church
Shaped like an abstract ship, music recitals are held here from June to August. *Map B3 • Open 10am–5pm daily • Charge for recitals*

10 Glanni
A pretty cascade over black lava on the Norðurá salmon river near Bifröst. You can see salmon as they head upstream. *Map C4*

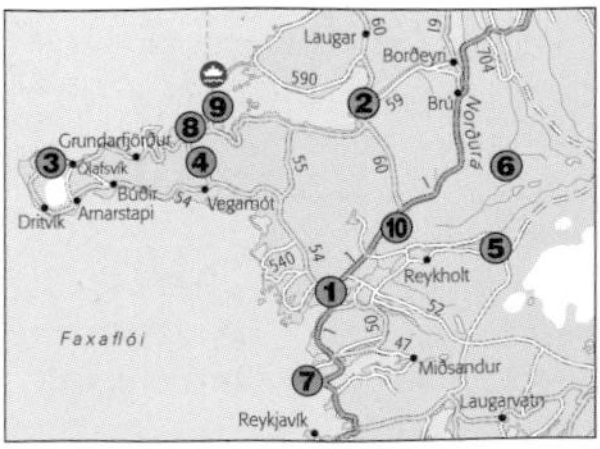

Price Categories

For a three course meal for one (without alcohol), with taxes and extra charges.

k	under ISK3,000
kk	ISK3,000–5,000
kkk	ISK5,000–7,000
kkkk	ISK7,000–9,000
kkkkk	over ISK9,000

Left **Restaurant at Hótel Hamar**

TOP 10 Places to Eat

1 Hótel Búðir
Probably western Iceland's finest diner, it focuses on fresh lamb and seafood dishes served in a smart setting. It is cheaper than similar Reykjavík venues *(see p130)*. *Map A4 • kkkk*

2 Hótel Hamar
Less formal than the Búðir but with a similar menu and exceptional vistas out over the sea. The attached bar has a balcony with more views *(see p130)*. *Map B4 • kkkk*

3 Settlement Centre
Great for an inexpensive meal – either the catch of the day, the lunch special of soup, salad and bread, or filling pasta dishes. Interesting vegetarian options too. *Map B4 • Brákarbraut 13–15, Borgarnes • 437 1600 • Open summer: 10am–9pm daily • kkk*

4 Hyrnan Snack Bar
Popular alternative to the ever-crowded Shell petrol station canteen, this is a place to grab a sandwich or a pizza in the adjacent shopping centre. *Map B4 • Brúartorg, Borgarnes • k*

5 Fosshótel Reykholt
The top place to eat in Reykholt, though in truth there's not much choice. The menu offers straightforward soups and grills; guests at the hotel also get to use the outdoor hot tubs. *Map C4 • 320 Reykholt • 435 1260 • kkkk • www.fosshotel.is*

6 Hótel Hellissandur
Within sight of Snæfellsnes' slopes, this hotel restaurant provides Icelandic staples such as fish of the day and burgers, excellent coffee and cakes. The bar is open until late. *Map A3 • Klettisbúð 9, Hellissandur • 430 8600 • kkk • www.hotelhellissandur.is*

7 Hótel Glymur
Smart retreat with an equally accomplished menu – carpaccio beef, pan seared trout and home-made ice cream. The café serves tasty snacks. Beautiful rural setting. *Map C3 • Hvalfjörður • 430 3100 • kkkk • www.hotelglymur.is*

8 Fjöruhúsið
Small café with good-value meals – especially famous for fish soup, coffee, home-made cakes and great harbour views. *Map A4 • Hellnar, Snæfellsnes • 435 6844 • Open Jun–Nov: 10am–9pm daily • kk*

9 Plássið
Hearty, tasty pizzas, burgers and grills, plus a well-stocked bar await at this welcoming retreat near the Stykkishólmur harbour. *Map B3 • Frúarstíg 1, Stykkishólmur • 436 1600 • kkk • www.plassid.is*

10 Narfeyrarstofa
The older wooden building with a tiny lounge and comfortable sofas gives it an edge. Try the Icelandic blue mussels and the home-made rhubarb cake. *Map B3 • Aðalgata 3, Stykkishólmur • 438 1119 • kkkk • www.narfeyrarstofa.is*

STAKK
6698
VALUR
5904

Left **Dynjandi falls** Right **Church in Hrafnseyri**

The West Fjords

THERE IS IMMENSE GRANDEUR *in the high, flat-topped mountains, brilliant blue seas and rugged coastline of the West Fjords, located on the extreme northwest of Iceland. For the region's scattered communities, life has been tough given the minimal infrastructure outside Ísafjörður, the only sizeable town. Attractions are mostly strung along the Fjords' west coast between Látrabjarg bird cliffs and Ísafjörður. Though the eastern Strandir coast offers its own low-key beauty, all inland views are filled by snow-streaked plateaus. It is best to visit in summer when the roads are open: you can fly into Ísafjörður but from there you will need to drive further.*

Látrabjarg landscape

TOP 10 Sights

1. Flókalundur
2. Patreksfjörður
3. Rauðasandur
4. Látrabjarg Bird Cliffs
5. Hólmavík Museum of Sorcery and Witchcraft
6. Hrafnseyri
7. Ísafjörður
8. Súðavík Arctic Fox Centre
9. Norðurfjörður
10. Drangajökull

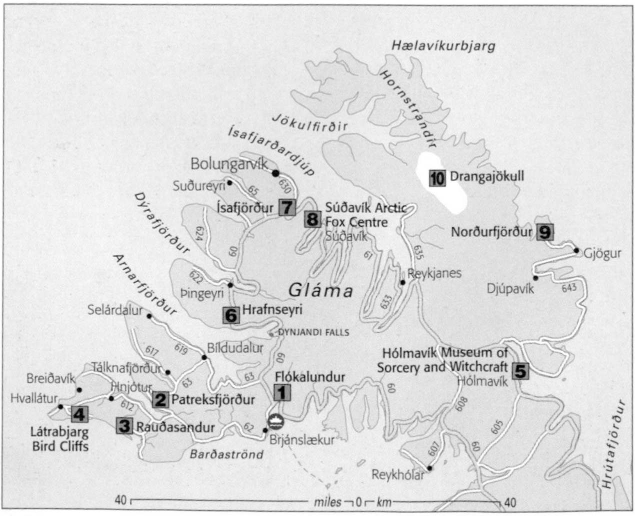

Preceding pages **Northeastern town of Húsavík**

1 Flókalundur

Flókalundur ("Flóki's Wood") is a tiny south-coast community on Route 62, named after the Viking Flóki Vilgerðarson. He endured a harsh winter here around AD 860 and, and on climbing nearby Lónfell, he saw the fjord below choked with ice and gave "Ice Land" its name. The surrounding wetlands, dwarf forest and barren basalt highlands are now protected as the Vatnsfjörður National Park, which you can explore using Hótel Flókalundur *(see p91)* as a summertime base. The hotel also runs a small store, fuel pump, campsite and restaurant. *Map B2*
• Vatnsfjörður National Park: www.ust.is

2 Patreksfjörður

Named after St Patrick, this comparatively sizeable fishing village on Route 62 is where Iceland's trawling industry kicked off from in the early 20th century. Patreksfjörður is famous for attacks by Basque pirates during the early 17th century. It is also the last place to stock up with provisions and fuel if you are heading to the Látrabjarg bird cliffs or the fantastic beach at Breiðavík *(see p23)*, southwest across the fjord at the end of Route 62. *Map A2*

3 Rauðasandur

Seals are frequently seen at this cinnamon-coloured beach at

Rauðasandur Beach

the southwesternmost peninsula of West Fjords, along the unsealed Route 614. Arctic skuas nest on the grasslands behind the spit – don't go too close or you may get a sharp peck on the head. The stone ruins of Sjöundá farm lie 5 km (3 miles) to the east of the beach. Gunnarson's novel, *Svartfugl (Blackbird)* is based on a double murder that took place at the farm in 1802. A steep and slippery track leads to sea views from Skor's high cliffs. *Map A3*

4 Látrabjarg Bird Cliffs

Látrabjarg is among the most stirring sights of Iceland, with millions of seabirds crammed into the tall cliffs throughout the summer – the noise and stench are remarkable in itself. The dramatic landscape, empty beaches and isolated buildings evoke visions of the hardships of rural life. Local buses make day trips to Látrabjarg during the summer months *(see pp22–3)*.

A view of Patreksfjörður village

Timber from the Sea

Iceland has always been short of home-grown timber for building boats and houses, which from Viking times has placed great demand on driftwood. Fortunately, plenty washes up around the country, particularly along the West Fjords' pebbly Strandir Coast, whose beaches are often strewn with tree trunks which have floated in from Siberia.

5 Hólmavík Museum of Sorcery and Witchcraft

A shrimp port on the southeast coast, Hólmavík has a Museum of Sorcery and Witchcraft which draws on the district's reputation for the dark arts – during the 17th century 20 witches (only one was female) were burned at the stake. The museum has models, trinkets, an audio tour and a live demonstration of spell-casting. They run a "Sorcerer's Cottage" 40 km (25 miles) up the coast, a reconstruction of the 20th-century shepherd dwellings. *Map C2 • Höfðagata 8, 510 Hólmavík • 897 6525, 451 3525 • Open 1 Jun–15 Sep: 9am–6pm daily • Adm • www.galdrasyning.is*

6 Hrafnseyri

Hrafnseyri – a church and turf farmhouse overlooking the sea at Arnarfjörður – is of great importance as it is the birthplace of Jón Sigurðsson (1811–79), whose

Windmill on Vigur Island

campaign for Iceland's independence from Denmark saw the parliament restored and a self-governing constitution enacted. His birthday, 17 June, is celebrated as National Day. The farmhouse is now a museum. Don't miss the dramatic Dynjandi waterfalls, 15 km (9 miles) to the south. *Map B2 • 456 8260 • Open Jun–Aug: 10am–6pm daily • Adm • www.hrafnseyri.is*

7 Ísafjörður

The region's main town and the only one with an airport, Ísafjörður is a likeable place with narrow streets and old buildings. Chief among these is the Turnhús *(see p63)*, overshadowed by the steep slopes of Kirkjubólsfjall. Across Ísafjarðardjúp straits, the uninhabited Hornstrandir Peninsula offers the ultimate hiking challenge. Boats run out here and to little Vigur island *(see p52)* through the summer. *Map B2 • Tourist office: 450 8060, www.isafjordur.is*

Bust of Jón Sigurðsson at Hrafnseyri

8 Súðavík Arctic Fox Centre

Originally the only mammal in Iceland was the Arctic fox, which probably drifted from Greenland on ice floes. Larger than the European fox, the Arctic fox has a dark blue summer coat (which turns white in winter) and lives on ground-nesting birds. This centre, 20 km (12 miles) around the coast from Ísafjörður at Eyrardalur farm, explores the Arctic fox's biology and relationship with man. ✆ *Map B2 • Eyrardal, Súðavík • 456 4922 • Open Jun–Aug: 9am–10pm daily • Adm • www.arcticfoxcenter.com*

9 Norðurfjörður

Just at the end of Route 648 up the east Strandir coast, Norðurfjörður is a small place, even for the West Fjords, but the scenery is stunning and makes the drive along loose gravel roads worthwhile. The town is backed by the 646-m- (2,125-ft-) high Krossnesfjall and looks out to sea across Norðurfjörður Bay, a lonely but romantic location. About 4 km (2 miles) around the coast lies Krossneslaug, a great beachside swimming pool, fed by a hot spring. ✆ *Map C2*

10 Drangajökull

The area's sole permanent icecap, Drangajökull is fairly remote, but makes a splendid sight on the top of a high plateau. During the 18th century it covered local farms but has now shrunk. The best close-up view is along the dead-end Route 635 to Kaldalónsjökull, a glacier descending off larger Drangajökull. It is an hour's walk from Kaldalón. ✆ *Map B2*

Drangajökull icecap, Hornstrandir

A Day in the West Fjords

Morning

Arriving at **Brjánslækur** by ferry from Stykkishólmur on the Snæfellsness Peninsula *(see pp78–81)*, drive north up Route 62 to **Flókalundur** *(see p87)*, fuel up and buy something for a picnic lunch here before turning on to Route 60. This good gravel road climbs up to the Dynjandisheiði Plateau and then drops abruptly to the coast at the stunning and noisy **Dynjandi** waterfall *(see p33)*, a great place to stretch your legs and spend an hour exploring the multi-level cascades (the lighting is best here in the evening). A grassy area at the foot of the falls makes a perfect spot for a picnic.

Afternoon

Leaving Dynjandi waterfalls, carry on around the bay to **Hrafnseyri**, birthplace of Jón Sigurðsson *(see p31)*, and drop in at the museum celebrating the life of this great Icelandic patriot. From here it is a further 65 km (40 miles) to **Ísafjörður** via Þingeyri, the West Fjords' oldest trading town, two mountain passes and a lengthy single-lane tunnel – there are passing bays inside, but traffic is never heavy. Once at Ísafjörður, track down your accommodation and then visit the **Maritime Museum** inside the antique **Turnhús** or simply stroll the handfull of streets down to the harbour, where you can usually spot marine ducks. The nearby **Faktorshús** *(see p91)* is an ideal place for a late afternoon coffee and cake.

Left **Traditional fishermen's houses at Ósvör Museum** Right **A view of Breiðavik Bay**

TOP 10 Best of the Rest

1 Pennugil

This narrow canyon on the Penná river is about a 30-minute walk from Flókalundur on a marked trail, with a bathable hot spring feeding it nearby. *Map B2*

2 Reiðskörð

Route 62 runs past this tall and fragmented volcanic dyke at Barðaströnd, the bay south of the West Fjords. *Map A3*

3 Brautarholt

Self-taught artist Samúel Jónsson (1884–1969) lived in this isolated valley at the end of Route 619, and created a bizarre range of sculptures and buildings. *Map A2 • Selárdalur, Arnarfjörður*

4 Skrúður

Set at the foot of a valley on Route 624, Iceland's oldest botanical garden was founded in 1909 by Reverend Sigtryggur Guðlaugsson. *Map A2 • Núpur*

5 Bolungarvík

This weatherbeaten fishing port is worth a trip to look at turf buildings and wooden fishing boats at the Ósvör Museum. The Natural History Museum showcases local stuffed birds. *Map B1 • Ósvör Museum: 892 5744, 456 7005, open by appointment, www.osvor.is; Natural History Museum: 456 7507, www.nabo.is*

6 Djúpavík

Wild and beautiful Djúpavík, halfway along Strandir's lonely coast, is dominated by a century-old shipwreck and a defunct herring processing factory. *Map C2*

7 Reykjanes

The hamlet of Reykjanes, a detour on Route 61 east from Ísafjörður, has a geothermal pool and sauna. *Map B2*

8 Kaldalón

Kaldalón ("Cold Lagoon") is fed by Drangajökull glacier *(see p89)*. It inspired local musician Sigvaldi Stefánsson (1881–1946) to call himself Kaldalóns. *Map B2*

9 Hælavíkurbjarg

This vertical, 258m- (847 ft-) high cliff between Hælavík and Hornvík islets, along with Látrabjarg and Hornbjarg, is one of the area's major bird colonies. *Map B1*

10 Hvallátur

Iceland's westernmost settlement comprises a farm and hotel at Breiðavík beach. It played a central role in the *Dhoon* shipwreck rescue *(see p23)*. *Map A2 • www.breidavik.is*

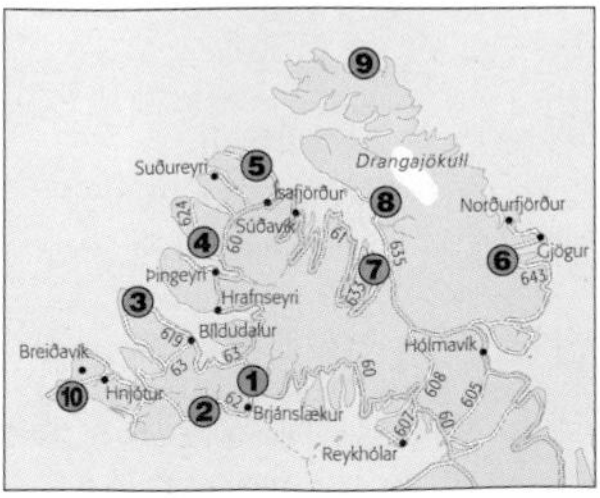

Price Categories		
For a three course meal for one (without alcohol), with taxes and extra charges.	k	under ISK3,000
	kk	ISK3,000–5,000
	kkk	ISK5,000–7,000
	kkkk	ISK7,000–9,000
	kkkkk	over ISK9,000

Left **Restaurant in Hótel Ísafjörður**

TOP 10 Places to Eat

1 Hótel Ísafjörður

This hotel's restaurant, Við Pollinn, has a Nordic decor and offers tasty, local standbys such as the catch of the day, grilled lamb and seafood soup *(see p130)*. *Map B2 • 456 3360 • kkkk*

2 Faktorshús

A great old wooden building that once housed Ísafjörður's trading manager, is now a hotel and café serving snacks and cakes. The location in an old part of town adds atmosphere. *Map B2 • Hæsti Kampstaður, Ísafjörður • 899 0742 • kk*

3 Hamraborg Snack Bar

This DVD rental and fast-food place serves burgers, sandwiches, pizza and *pylsur* (hot dogs) with remoulade, onions and tomato sauce. *Map B2 • Hafnarstræti 7, Ísafjörður • 456 3166 • k*

4 Hótel Flókalundur

Small restaurant has a pricey evening menu (order ahead) with well-prepared seafood and game dishes. Better value, set lunch cafeteria-type specials. *Map A2 • Vatnsfirði 451, Patreksfjörður • 456 2011 • Open 20 May–20 Sep • kk–kkk • www.flokalundur.is*

5 Hótel Laugarhóll

Pleasant hotel in a marvellous setting with a thermal pool and hiking trails within walking distance. Its excellent restaurant has set and à la carte menus. *Map B3 • Klúka, Strandir, Bjarnarfjörður • 451 3380 • kkkk • www.laugarholl.is*

6 Hótel Djúpavík

Another friendly place in a fantastic location, this hotel serves tasty, home-cooked food in its cosy, wood-beamed dining room. *Map C2 • Djúpavík, Strandir • 451 4037 • kkk • www.djupavik.com*

7 Café Riis

The best restaurant on the Strandir coast, with pan-fried puffin breast, roast trout and lamb fillets served with panache. Also provides sandwiches, burgers, cakes and coffee. *Map C2 • Hafnarbraut 39, Hólmavík • 451 3567 • kkk*

8 Hótel Bjarkalundur

If you are driving in or out of the West Fjords along Route 60, then the welcoming restaurant at the otherwise insignificant Hótel Bjarkalundur will be very welcome. *Map B3 • Reykhólahreppi • 894 1295 • kkk • http://bjarkalundur.is*

9 Hótel Flatey

Simple but well-prepared lamb and fish dishes at reasonable prices given the remote location on an island in the bay between Snæfellsnes and West Fjords. *Map B3 • Flatey, Breiðafjörður • 422 7610 • kkkk • www.hotelflatey.is*

10 Þorpið

Good grill restaurant serving the usual fare, but the seafood is above average, which it should be given the town's great seafaring heritage. *Map A2 • Aðalstræti 73, Patreksfjörður • 456 1295 • kk*

Left **Boiling mud pool in the Hverir area, Lake Mývatn** Right **Hraun í Öxnadalur farm**

North Iceland

RICH IN HISTORY AND WILDLIFE *and with an amazing landscape, North Iceland could easily make for a week-long trip. There is the pleasant regional capital, Akureyri, with its fjord setting and old buildings; a glut of birds and volcanic attractions around Lake Mývatn; Húsavík's laid-back charm, unusual museums and whale-watching cruises; Jökulsárgljúfur's incredible gorge system and waterfalls; not to mention a wealth of antique farms, churches and saga sites, some of them – such as Hólar – central to Icelandic culture. Almost everything is located on or easy to reach from Route 1.*

Top 10 Sights

1. Blönduós
2. Sauðárkrókur
3. Hraun í Öxnadalur
4. Dalvík
5. Akureyri
6. Hólar
7. Húsavík
8. Lake Mývatn
9. Jökulsárgljúfur
10. Dettifoss

Detail of the altar at Hólar Church

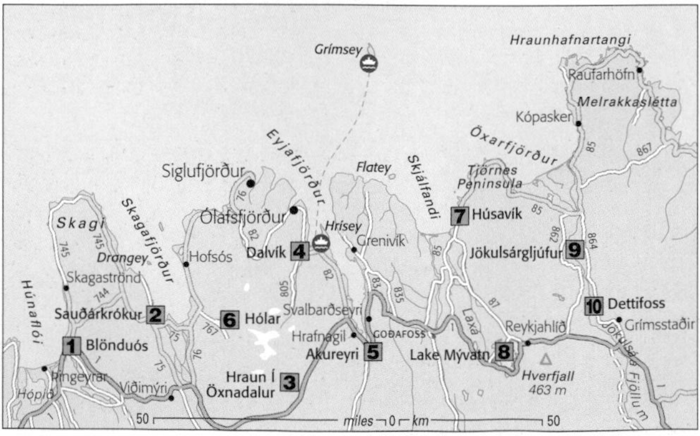

1 Blönduós

The most striking thing about this small riverside fishing port and regional service centre on Húnaflói Bay is its extraordinary church, consecrated in 1993, whose steeply sloping concrete walls echo the shape of the mountains nearby. The acoustics are good too, if you are lucky enough to catch the choir performing. Other attractions include trips to see seals and birdlife in the bay and, 15 km (9 miles) west at Vatnsdalshólar, an expanse of strange mounds formed during an earthquake, site of Iceland's last execution in 1830. *Map D2*

2 Sauðárkrókur

Approached from a lush valley, Sauðárkrókur's appeal comes from the tiny knot of atmospheric old buildings that surround the town "square", principally the church and Hótel Tindastóll (www.hoteltindastoll.com), which are said to be haunted. The coast here features in *Grettir's Saga*, including the sheer-sided Drangey island, where Grettir spent his last years as an outlaw; and Grettislaug, a lovely seaside thermal bathing pool where he recovered after swimming over from the island in search of fresh embers to reignite his own fire. *Map D2*

• Drangey boat trips with Viggó Jónsson, 821 0090, May–Aug, www.drangey.net

Street in the old part of Sauðárkrókur

3 Hraun í Öxnadalur

This non-descript farm by the roadside in the deep, glacier-carved Ox Valley is famous as the birthplace of poet and biologist Jónas Hallgrímsson (1807–1845). Hallgrímsson's romantic verses extolling the landscape influenced the way Icelanders, most of whom then lived poor lives in rural turf buildings, began to perceive their country as glorious rather than embarrassing. He is one of the two people honoured with burial at Þingvellir Church *(see p8)*. *Map E2*

4 Dalvík

Dalvík is a small port with an unusual Fish Soup Festival *(see p54)* and boats to Grímsey island *(see pp52–3)*, and also serves as a jump-off point for ferries to the ptarmigan-rich Hrísey island. The nearby Svarfaðadalur Valley is great for hiking. Though most of the set trails are lengthy, you can also spend just a couple of hours strolling or picking whortleberries during August. *Map E2*

Dalvík port with mountains in the background

Grettir's Saga

Grettir's Saga recounts the life of Grettir Ásmundarson, a fierce warrior who performs great deeds in the service of others, but is haunted by a *draugur* or evil ghost. Grettir ends his life as an outlaw on Drangey island, where he is finally killed by his enemies.

5 Akureyri

Iceland's largest settlement after Reykjavík with a population of over 17,000, Akureyri is a relaxed town with a pretty harbour and lots of shops, cafés and restaurants. Looming over everything is Akureyrarkirkja, the huge church, with excellent stained-glass windows (some brought from England's old Coventry cathedral) and some modern depictions of famous Icelanders. Do not miss the Botanical Gardens, where both native and imported plants thrive, or the Viking-age burial remains at the Akureyri Museum. *Map E2 • Tourist Info: www.visitakureyri.is; Akureyri Museum: Aðalstræti 58, 462 4162 (winter), 571 1830 (summer), www.minjasafnid.is*

6 Hólar

More fully known as Hólar í Hjaltadal, this was once the largest settlement in northern Iceland thanks to the monastery and religious school founded in 1106 by bishop Jón Ögmundsson, which attracted scholars and monks from across Europe. These institutions survived the Reformation – which saw the execution of Hólar's last Catholic bishop, Jón Arason – and today the cathedral *(see p66)* and the college specializing in aquaculture, rural tourism and horse science are the sole buildings here. *Map D2 • Tourist office: 455 6300; open summer: 8am–10pm; www2.holar.is*

Akureyrarkirkja (Akureyri Cathedral)

Whale-watching, Húsavík

7 Húsavík

A delightful town overlooking the wide Skjálfandi Bay, Húsavík is Iceland's whale-watching capital, with several daily tours throughout summer. There is also the superb Whale Museum and an informative museum in the town library. The coast makes for some good walks along grassy headlands and little beaches from where you might see seals. *Map E2 • Whale watching tours: www.gentlegiants.is and www.northsailing.is*

8 Lake Mývatn

Whether you have come to Iceland to climb cinder cones, hike over steaming expanses of solidified lava, bathe in open-air geothermal pools, see hot mud pools, make a day-trip into the stark interior deserts or simply spend time bird-watching, you will find it all at Lake Mývatn. Although many sights are spread around the lakeshore, you will need a vehicle to reach the outlying attractions which include a flooded volcano crater known as "Hell" *(see pp16–17)*.

9 Jökulsárgljúfur

Set in a northern segment of the massive Vatnajökull National Park *(see pp18–19)*, this mighty canyon is excellent for hiking, following the top of the gorge or cutting across a land rich in flowers and birdlife. Sights along the way include striking red formations at Rauðhólar, twisted hexagonal granite columns at Hljóðaklettar, Hólmatungur's springs and Dettifoss *(see p32)*. *Map F2 • National Park: www.ust.is*

10 Dettifoss

Part of the attraction of visiting this waterfall is the effort needed to get there, as the roads are rough gravel and open only for a few months each year. The eastern approach is easiest and traverses a stony volcanic plateau, with mountains in the distance. There is a detour well worth taking to Hafragilsfoss, another splendid waterfall just downstream with a viewpoint inside the dramatic Jökulsárgljúfur canyon *(see p32)*. *Map F2*

Visitors at Dettifoss, Jökulsárgljúfur

A Day in the Lake Mývatn Area

Morning

Start early, and you can just about pack all of **Lake Mývatn**'s attractions *(see pp16–17)* into one long summer day. Begin with the subterranean hot pools at **Grjótagjá**, then move south to tackle **Hverfjall**'s slippery black slopes, making a circuit of the rim for spectacular views of the whole Mývatn area. Back at ground level, **Dimmuborgir** presents an extraordinary maze of natural lava sculptures (look for rare gyrfalcons nesting on rocky towers here), with only a short drive to the lakeshore at **Höfði Nature Park**, where you will definitely encounter numerous species of waterfowl, including barrow's goldeneye, scaup and mergansers. Follow the road to the south side of the lake at **Skútustaðir**, home to a large group of grassy pseudocraters.

Afternoon

Depending on your progress, you can grab lunch at the Dimmuborgir or Skútustaðir cafés, or circuit the lake to Reykjahlíð's **Gamli Bærinn**. Head east to the fearsome **Námaskarð** mud pits, set in a wasteland full of steam and eye-watering smells. A good side road runs north from here, via the Leirbotn Power Station, to where Víti volcano overlooks **Leirhnjúkur**, a huge expanse of steaming lava laid down in the 1980s – a place for careful exploration. Round off the day with a good soak on the way home at the **Jarðböðin** nature baths.

Left **Goðafoss** Right **Turf-roofed old farmhouse at Laufás**

TOP 10 Best of the Rest

1 Hofsós

Visit the Iceland Emigration Museum *(see p62)*, one of the oldest Icelandic timber houses *(Pakkhúsið)*, and have a dip in the wonderful pool *(see p51)*.

2 Glaumbær

Classic turf farmhouses built between 1750 and 1879. The use of imported timber hints at the family's comparative wealth. *Map D2 • Glaumbær, 556 Varmahlíð • 453 6173 • Open 1 Jun–10 Sep: 9am–6pm daily • Adm • www.skagafjordur.is*

3 Goðafoss

This impressive waterfall is named after events that occured when Christianity was introduced here in AD 1000 *(see p33)*.

4 Vaglaskógur

This beautiful, extensive stretch of birch woodland along Fnjóskadalur Valley is a popular camping area with a small store and walking trails. *Map E2 • Campsite open May–Sep; 860 2213*

5 Laufás

The museum here, housed in a 19th-century turf farmhouse, displays period household objects. The adjacent church is a little older with a 17th-century pulpit. *Map E2 • 463 3196 • Open 1 Jun–15 Sep: 10am–6pm daily • Adm*

6 Grenjaðarstaður

Some of the buildings here have flowers on their turf roofs. Check out the headstones carved with runes in the cemetery. *Map E2 • 464 3688 • Open Jun–Aug: 10am–6pm daily • Adm*

7 Laxá í Aðaldal

Better known for its fishing potential further downstream, the Laxá's turbulent flow as it exits Lake Mývatn is a magnet for red-necked phalarope, barrow's goldeneye and harlequin duck *(see p64)*.

8 Þingeyrarkirkja

Built between 1909 and 1911, this remarkable church sits alone on a vegetated sandbar *(see p67)*. *Map C2 • Þingeyrar, near Blönduós • 895 4473 • Open Jun–Aug: 10am–5pm daily • Adm*

9 Hvítserkur

The natural rock formation resembling a 15-m (49-ft) tall dinosaur drinking from the sea, lies on the east of the Vatnsnes Peninsula on Route 711. *Map C4*

10 Tjörnes

This rounded peninsula with distinct banded geological strata yields bivalve and plant fossils. A signposted fossil bed is located near Ytri-Tunga farm. *Map E2*

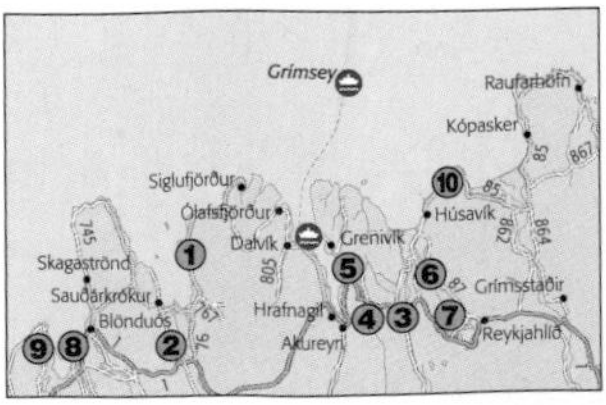

Price Categories	
For a three course meal for one (without alcohol), with taxes and extra charges.	**k** under ISK3,000
	kk ISK3,000–5,000
	kkk ISK5,000–7,000
	kkkk ISK7,000–9,000
	kkkkk over ISK9,000

Left **The restaurant at Hótel Gígur**

TOP 10 Places to Eat

1 Hótel KEA
Owned by the company that built Akureyri, this restaurant in Hótel KEA *(see p130)* offers everything from lunch buffets to à la carte dining. The wooden interior is dimly lit. *kkkk*

2 Gamli Bærinn
The café-bar in Hótel Reynihlíð serves beer, light meals, snacks and coffee through the day. Gamli Bærinn's hearty traditional lamb soup is legendary. *Map F2 • Reykjahlíð, Mývatn • 464 4170 • Open May–Aug: 10am–midnight daily • kkk*

3 Hótel Gígur
This hotel restaurant *(see p130)* has a beautiful setting with views out over the pseudocraters on Mývatn's southern shore. Serves local fish and lamb. *Map F3*

4 Staðarskáli
On the highway, halfway on the long drive between Reykjavík and Akureyri, pull up at this roadhouse to stretch your legs over coffee and a burger. *Map C3 • Vegamót, Hrútafjörður • 440 1336 • k*

5 Bautinn
Unpretentious restaurant that has been around for a long time and serves reliably tasty grilled beef, lamb and seafood main courses. *Map E2 • Hafnarstræti 92, Akureyri • 462 1818 • kkk*

6 Bláa Kannan
Unmistakable corrugated iron exterior painted dark blue, with tables spilling on to the street, this is your best bet in town for coffee, cake and people-watching. *Map E2 • Hafnarstræti 96, Akureyri • 461 4600 • Open summer: 8:30am–11:30pm, winter: 9am–11:30pm • kk*

7 Hótel Blönduós
The restaurant at this hotel offers tasty, fresh Icelandic home-made food, including lamb steak, codfish, herring and rhubarb crumble. *Map D2 • Aðalgata 6, 540 Blönduós • 452 4205 • kkk*

8 Gamli Baukur
Set inside restored wooden warehouses overlooking the harbour, this snug place serves excellent soups and fresh fish daily, all at a very reasonable cost given the size of the portions. *Map E2 • Harbour, Húsavík • 464 2442 • Open noon–8pm Sun–Wed, noon–1am Thu, noon–3am Fri & Sat • kk*

9 Salka
Offering competition to the nearby Gamli Baukur, this restaurant has a similar menu but with the bonus of outdoor tables when there is sunshine, at least. *Map E2 • Garðarsbraut 6, Húsavík • 464 2551 • kkk*

10 Greifinn
A no-nonsense pizza restaurant, with an extensive menu. It is also a nice place to sit and eat if you do not fancy take-away. *Map E2 • Glerágata 20, Akureyri • 460 1600 • Open 11:30am–9:30pm Sun–Thu, 11:30am–11pm Fri & Sat • k*

Left **Turf house at Bakkagerði** Right **Lagarfljót river near Egilsstaðir**

East Iceland

EAST ICELAND COVERS A VARIED REGION *of broad river valleys, boggy plateaus surrounding the mighty Vatnajökull icecap, and a dramatically compressed coastline forming the East Fjords. The main centres are Egilsstaðir on the shores of forested Lake Lögurinn and Höfn, a springboard for the main Vatnajökull National Park. Visiting smaller communities such as Vopnafjörður, Bakkagerði and Seyðisfjörður (with its international ferry) provides an insight into the daily life here, while rewarding side-trips include a visit to Papey island or the remote Kárahnjúkar hydro dam.*

Puffins on Papey island

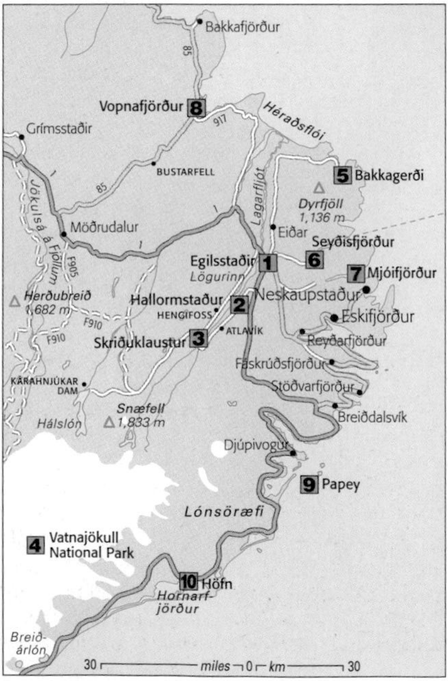

Top 10 Sights

1. Egilsstaðir
2. Hallormsstaður
3. Skriðuklaustur
4. Vatnajökull National Park
5. Bakkagerði (Borgafjörður eystri)
6. Seyðisfjörður
7. Mjóifjörður
8. Vopnafjörður
9. Papey
10. Höfn

1 Egilsstaðir

Just east of the elongated Lake Lögurinn, Egilsstaðir lies at the junction with Route 1 and several smaller roads radiating coastwards to the scattered East Fjord communities. An unpretentious service centre with a variety of accommodation, restaurants and well-stocked shops. Attractions include the East Iceland Museum, featuring a Viking burial site and reconstructed traditional turf houses; and the 70-km (44-mile) drive around Lögurinn to take in saga sites, extensive woodlands and one of Iceland's tallest waterfalls. *Map G3 • Summer-only buses from Akureyri and Reykjavík via Höfn. Airport open year-round • Museum: open Jun–Sep: 11am–5pm daily, adm*

2 Hallormsstaður

Southwest of Egilsstaðir, lakeshore Hallormsstaður sits beside Iceland's most extensive forest, grown since the 1900s for recreational use and for timber. A web of wooded walking trails heads up the valley slopes, while a roadside Forestry Office has a small arboretum with 40 tree species as well as Iceland's tallest, a 22-m- (62-ft-) high larch. Near the lake is pretty Atlavík Bay with scented birch surrounding the camping ground. *Map G3*

Egilsstaðir town, near Lake Lögurinn

3 Skriðuklaustur

This imposing stone-built villa belonging to author Gunnar Gunnarsson (1889–1975) sits on Lögurinn's western shore, close to the church at Valþjófstaður, Hengifoss, and the road to Kárahnjúkar. Gunnar's series of novels about Icelandic farm life, *Af Borgslægtens Historie*, were later filmed. Besides being a Visitor Centre for Vatnajökull National Park, there is a gallery here that hosts regular exhibitions. The attached Klausturkaffi offers a coffee buffet with home-made cakes. *Map G3 • 471 2990 • Open May–Sep: noon–5pm daily; Oct–Apr: open occasionally, call in advance • www.skriduklaustur.is*

4 Vatnajökull National Park

The bulk of Europe's largest national park surrounds the Vatnajökull icecap itself, whose eastern fringes are 100 km (62 miles) southwest of Egilsstaðir or 10 km (6 miles) northwest from Höfn. Direct access points include the Kárahnjúkur road west of Egilsstaðir, for which you will need a 4WD, or hiking tracks through Lónsöræfi Reserve *(see p102)*. Skidoo trips from Höfn will get you to the ice and the various glacier tongues can also be viewed from here *(see pp18–19)*. *Map F4*

A view of the Vatnajökull icecap

Héraðsflói's Birdlife

Héraðsflói – a broad bay with black-sand beach and boggy meadows inland along the myriad streamlets of the Jökulsá á Brú river – makes a superb place for observing birdlife. Look for marine ducks (including the long-tailed or old squaw and scoter), godwit, red-throated divers and even hobbys, Iceland's smallest bird of prey.

5 Bakkagerði (Borgafjörður eystri)

Part of the fun of visiting Bakkagerði, East Fjord's most endearing settlement, is the journey via the Héraðsflói estuary's grassy lagoons and steep ranges that isolate the village. On arrival you will find a tiny community backed by jagged Dyrfjöll mountain, with sights including a little hummock near the church named Álfaborg, home to Iceland's fairy queen, and a sizeable puffin colony overlooking the fishing harbour. Superb, lengthy hiking trails lead south to Seyðisfjörður. *Map H2*

6 Seyðisfjörður

Seyðisfjörður's charm lies in its steep fjord setting and 19th-century wooden architecture near the harbour. The church, several houses and two hotels are the

Church on Seyðisfjörður's main street

pick, most painted in pastel hues and originally imported from Norway. An important naval station during World War II and a herring port before then, today Seyðisfjörður is linked to Norway by the *Nörunna* ferry, which visits weekly in summer via the Faroes and Denmark. *Map H3*

7 Mjóifjörður

A long, thin inlet accessed by the gravel Route 953, Mjóifjörður (Narrow Fjord) is worth the bumpy drive to Brekka village and the remote lighthouse at Dalatangi. The road between the shoreline and steep mountains offers some close-ups of beautiful streams and cascades, plus the chance of seeing the Arctic fox that are more at ease with humans in this remote area. *Map H3*

8 Vopnafjörður

If you are making the long coastal drive along Route 85 from Húsavík towards Egilsstaðir, set

Bakkagerði with the Dyrfjöll mountain in the background

aside an hour for Vopnafjörður, a small town built on a steep prong of land. It has a museum detailing the plight of local communities following the 1875 eruption of Víti at Askja *(see p39)*. An outdoor geothermal pool at Selárdalur and Bustarfell's immaculate collection of old turf farmhouses *(see p102)* are located close by. *Map G2*

9 Papey

The ferry ride to Papey is one of the highlights of East Iceland, taking in rock ledges full of snoozing seals, an ocean covered in seabirds flapping frantically out of the way of boats and the small, grass-topped island, thought to have been inhabited by monks before the Vikings arrived *(see p53)*. *Map H4*

Boats lined up at Höfn

10 Höfn

Höfn started as a warehouse during the 1860s, and has since developed into a small working port. The town makes a good base for trips to Vatnajökull National Park: the Glacier Exhibition fills you in on the area; you can book skiddoo trips and super-jeep tours to the icecap; while hikers can aim for Lónsöræfi Reserve. For glacier views, head for the landmark statue on the shore – avoiding the nearby Arctic tern colony. *Map G5 • Year-round buses to Reykjavík, and summer services to Egilsstaðir, airport open year-round*

A Day in East Iceland

Morning

Before starting on this 70-km (44-mile) circuit of **Lake Lögurinn** and the Lagarfljót Valley, climb the hillock behind the Menntaskólinn school in **Egilsstaðir** for a view of the region – on a clear day you can see southwest over the lake as far as **Snæfell** *(see p102)*, Iceland's highest free-standing peak. Then head south, branching off the highway onto Route 931 past fields full of lambs and Icelandic horses, until a surprising amount of woodland begins to spring up around **Hallormsstaður**, where you can explore walking tracks or the Forestry Office's arboretum, or take in lakeside views at **Atlavík**. Exiting the woods past Atlavík, the main road crosses the lake to Lögurinn's west shore, where you turn left and drive some distance to **Skriðuklaustur**.

Afternoon

After having a snack at Skriðuklaustur's café, **Klausturkaffi**, and a look at the National Park exhibition, continue south to **Valþófstaður** church with its reproduction of carved Viking doors, then retrace your route back past Skriðuklaustur to where the 60-km- (37-mile-) long Route 910 ascends to moorlands around Snæfell and the **Kárahnjúkar hydro dam** *(see p102)*. You need three hours for this round trip, otherwise follow an hour-long walking track uphill to **Hengifoss** *(see p102)* after parking your car. Stay on the western shore for the drive back to Egilsstaðir.

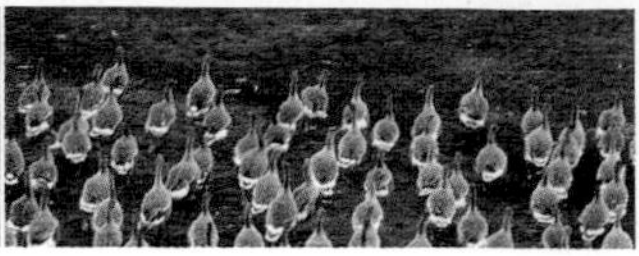

Left **Hengifoss, dropping into a gorge** Right **Flock of geese in a field, Eyjabakkar**

Top 10 Best of the Rest

1 Hengifoss

This 118-m (387-ft) fall is Iceland's third-highest, dropping in a narrow ribbon off a cliff-face layered in red and black. On the way up don't miss the twisted basalt columns at Litlifoss. *Map G3*

2 Steinasafn Petru

Extensive private geological collection, featuring coloured stones, crystals and mineral samples from all over the world. Owner does not speak English. *Map H4 • Sunnuhlíð, Stöðvarfjörður, East Fjords • 475 8834, 475 8839 • Open May–Sep: 9am–6pm daily • Adm*

3 Hvítserkur

Spectacular, orange, pink and grey rhyolite mountain 10 km (6 miles) along a hiking trail from Bakkagerði – the colours really stand out after rain. The trail is straightforward, but be prepared for changing weather. *Map H3*

4 Snæfell

This isolated, snow-capped granite core of an old volcano lies at Vatnajökull's north-east corner. It is located on a 4WD-only track. Hiking huts around the base. *Map F4 • www.vatnajokulsthjodgardur.is*

5 Kárahnjúkar Hydro Dam

Controversial project that dammed the Dimmugljúfur canyon to provide power for a smelter. The sealed road crosses highland tundra, full of reindeer. *Map F4*

6 Lónsöræfi

Wild, uninhabited area, rich in gorges, moorland and glacier scenery. An unmarked, 5-day trail for self-sufficient hikers runs from Stafafell to Snæfell. *Map G4 • www.vatnajokulsthjodgardur.is*

7 Eyjabakkar

Boggy highland region en route to Kárahnjúkar or Snæfell, it is a breeding ground for greylag geese and whooper swans; reindeer are common too.

8 Valþjófstaður

Farm and red-roofed church, with replica carved Viking panels as doors. The originals are in Reykjavík's National Museum. *Map G3 • Open 10am–5pm daily*

9 Djúpivogur Bulandsnes

Three beautiful fjords and a profusion of Icelandic wildlife make this area a nature-lover's paradise. *Map G4 • www.djupivogur.is*

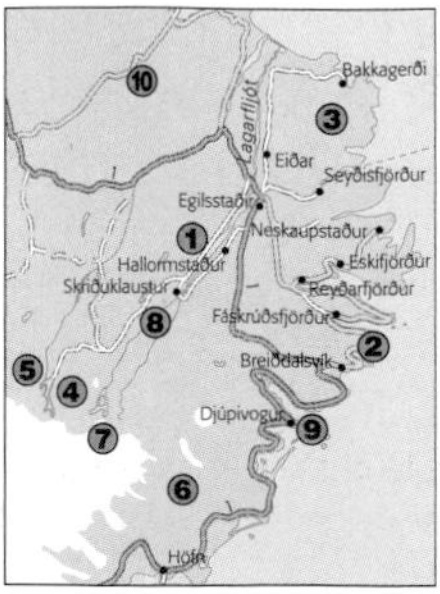

10 Bustarfell

Well-preserved turf-roofed farm-houses (rebuilt in 1770), occupied by the same family since 1532. Café on site. *Map G2 • 471 2211 • Open 10 Jun–10 Sep: 10am–5pm daily • Adm*

Price Categories		
For a three course meal for one (without alcohol), with taxes and extra charges.	k	under ISK3,000
	kk	ISK3,000–5,000
	kkk	ISK5,000–7,000
	kkkk	ISK7,000–9,000
	kkkkk	over ISK9,000

Left **Café Nielsen, Egilsstaðir**

TOP 10 Places to Eat

1 Fjallakaffi
This café is attached to the highest farm in Iceland, reached along Route 901 south off Route 1 from Lake Mývatn. Accommodation is also available. *Map F3 • Möðrudal á Fjöllum • 471 1858, 894 8181 • Open summer: 2–5pm daily • kk*

2 Hótel Hérað
Local reindeer steak is the obvious dish to try at Hérað's restaurant, although they also offer lamb and seafood dishes *(see p130). kkkk*

3 Café Nielsen
Located in an old wooden building, this restaurant-bar has an outdoor deck downstairs. Try the lunch buffets, soup and salad to keep the costs down. Grilled fish and lamb are excellent. *Map G3 • Tjarnarbraut 1, Egilsstaðir • 471 2626 • Open summer: 11:30am–11:30pm, 1pm–2am Fri & Sat; winter: 11:30am–10pm Mon–Thu, 1pm–1am Fri & Sat • kkkk*

4 Hótel Hallormstaður
Popular fixed-price lunches and dinner buffets of cold smoked lamb, bread and soup are served here in a nice setting. The service is friendly *(see p132). kk*

5 Klausturkaffi
Home-made wild mushroom soup, reindeer and goose dishes are the specialities at this café. The menu changes regularly. It is also renowned for its coffee and cakes. *Map G3 • Skriðuklaustur • 471 2992 • kkk*

6 Hótel Tangi
The hotel restaurant is the most popular place to eat in Vopnafjörður. Their pizzas, burgers and grilled fish are excellent. *Map G2 • Hafnarbyggð 17, Vopnafjörður • 473 1840 • kkk*

7 Hótel Aldan
Housed in a pretty, wooden building, the restaurant in this hotel is a great place to eat an early cooked breakfast or an elegant three-course dinner. Their fish dishes are outstanding *(see p132). kkkk*

8 Hótel Framtið
Fill up on hearty pasty, fish and lamb dishes at this eatery on Djúpivogur's harbour before making the trip over to Papey island *(see p130). kkk*

9 Álfacafé
Housed inside a former fish factory near Bakkagerði's old harbour, Álfacafé has exceptionally heavy tables and crockery made out of solid stone. Only light meals are served and their sandwiches are good. *Map H2 • Bakkagerði • 862 9802, 472 9900 • Open 11am–8pm daily • kk*

10 Kaffi Hornið
Warm up inside this timber building on Höfn's main street. Soup, pasta, pizza and grills, along with coffee and the inevitable cakes, are served on checkered tablecloths. *Map G5 • Hafnarbraut 42, Höfn • 478 2600 • kkk*

Left **Basalt cliffs near Vík** Right **Main bathing pool at the Blue Lagoon**

South Iceland

SOUTH ICELAND FORMS AN EXTRAORDINARILY RICH and long band of coastline, minor icecaps, fertile river plains and explosive volcanic landscapes, all wrapped up in history and folklore. The Blue Lagoon and the "Golden Circle," which includes Þingvellir, Geysir and Gullfoss, are Iceland's most iconic tourist sights. There is also the Hekla volcano, a wealth of saga locations, some waterfalls, access to hiking grounds at Landmannalaugar and Þórsmörk, the gem-like but often-overlooked Westman Islands and peaceful Vík village, all within easy reach from Reykjavík. East of Vík, you will need more time to reach Kirkjubæjarklaustur town, the Jökulsárlón glacial lagoon and the fringes of Vatnajökull National Park at Skaftafell and Höfn.

TOP 10 Sights

1. **Þingvellir National Park**
2. **Geysir**
3. **Gullfoss**
4. **The Blue Lagoon**
5. **Þjórsárdalur**
6. **Vestmannaeyjar**
7. **Markarfljót Valley**
8. **Vík**
9. **Kirkjubæjarklaustur**
10. **Jökulsárlón**

A view of the settlement at Vík

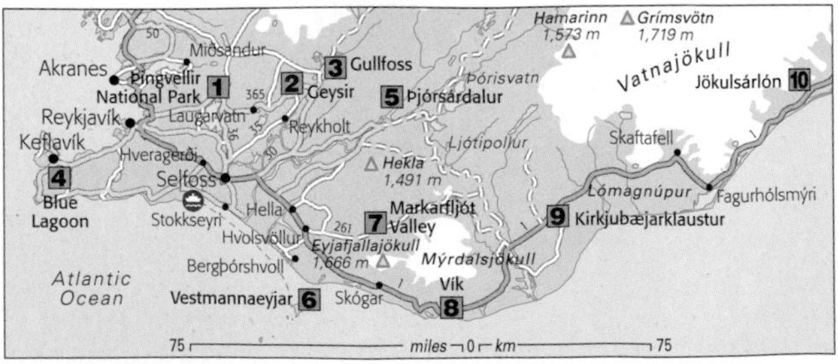

Preceding pages **Hiking in the Landmannalaugar area**

Gullfoss seen from the middle viewpoint

1 Þingvellir National Park

This amazing rift valley, now a UNESCO World Heritage site, was the setting for Iceland's open-air parliament in Viking times. Stop at the Visitor Centre on the way along Route 36 for superlative views over the rift walls and the lava plains. Spend a few minutes picking out key features such as the Law Rock, Þingvellir Church, Almannagjá canyon, Öxarárfoss, Þingvallavatn lake and the Skjaldbreiður volcano *(see pp8–9)*.

2 Geysir

It is incredible to find such a raw, primal sight as Geysir's scalding water spouts erupting by the side of the main road. Just 90 minutes from the capital, Geysir has a hotel, petrol station and tourist centre alongside. The key geysir to watch here is Strokkur, but if you are lucky the original vent, Geysir itself, might blow its top. The whole site is surrounded by a collection of smaller hot pools, each with its own distinct character *(see pp12–13)*.

3 Gullfoss

The final stop on a tour of the "Golden Circle", Gullfoss is Iceland's most dramatic waterfall and deafening, except in winter. Make sure you get a look from as many viewpoints as possible, especially from the top of the canyon, from where you can appreciate the Hvítá river's journey from the barren Interior to the north *(see pp14–15)*.

Hot pools of Blesi, Geysir

4 The Blue Lagoon

Iceland's southwest extreme, the Reykjanes Peninsula is almost entirely covered in barren lava fields, which makes finding the vivid Blue Lagoon hidden within it doubly surprising. Creative use of waste water from a geothermal power plant and the outdoor soak at the Blue Lagoon make for an outstanding experience. Its white silt is said to have health benefits too *(see pp10–11)*.

5 Þjórsárdalur

Þjórsárdalur is a broad, stark river valley, sterilized by a huge eruption in 1102 of the Hekla volcano, just one ridge away to the east. The eruption buried a Viking longhouse up the valley at Stöng, now excavated and open to the public via a rough, gravel track, with a full reconstruction nearby at Þjóðveldisbærinn. Up a parallel track, Þjórsárdalslaug is a great open-air pool, though, sadly, it is currently closed due to ashfall. *Map D5 • Both access roads subject to closure • Þjóðveldisbærinn: Jun–Aug: 10am–6pm daily, www.thjodveldisbaer.is; Þjórsárdalslaug: see www.swimminginiceland.com for latest information • Adm*

Njál's Saga

A gripping account of a bloody, 50-year-long family feud revolving around the household of Njáll Þorgeirsson, in which the evil schemings of Mörð Valgarðsson causes the deaths of both Njáll and his friend Gunnar Hámundarson. The hard-boiled delivery is softened by deadpan humour and vivid insights into daily life during Viking times.

6 Vestmannaeyjar

The Westman Islands are a string of volcanic outcrops off the south coast, which include the world's newest island, Surtsey *(see p53)*. Heimaey is the largest and only inhabited island in the group, famous for the1973 Eldfell eruption, which partially buried Heimaey town, almost ending its fishing industry. Stay overnight and climb Eldfell's still-steaming slopes, walk around the coast in half a day, visit the wooden Nordic church, look out for puffins or enjoy the Þjóðhátíð festival *(see p55)*. *Map C6 • Daily ferry from Þorlakshöfn, flights from Reykjavík & Bakki.*

7 Markarfljót Valley

To reach the pretty valley of Markarfljót, take Route 1 to Hvolsvöllur township – where you should visit the excellent

Hikers on a trail, Skaftafell National Park

Saga Centre – and then follow the 30-km- (19-mile-) long Route 261 east. The area is central to key scenes from *Njál's Saga*, including the farm Völlur, where the tale opens; and Hlíðarendi, home to the virtuous Gunnar Hámundarson. There is a church on the hillside at Hlíðarendi today, from where you can look seawards over the valley, where landmarks like rocky Stóri-Dímon stand proud. *Map D5 • Saga Centre: open Jun–15 Sep 9am–6pm daily, adm, www.njala.is*

8 Vík

This peaceful seafront community of around 300 people is located below Reynisfjall's tall cliffs, with a dramatic black-sand beach, great views west over the flat Mýrdalssandur, lively bird colonies and some towering offshore black stacks known as the Troll Rocks. Skógar and its waterfall are just up the road *(see p33)*. There are more sea-scapes west around the corner at Reynisfjall and Dyrhólaey *(see p34)*. Also close by are a number of walking tracks. All in all, this is a great place to chill out for a few days. *Map D6*

Black beach, west of Dyrhólaey

9 Kirkjubæjarklaustur

A tiny highway town in the middle of nowhere, Kirkjubæjarklaustur is surrounded by pseudocraters and hexagonal lava pavements known as Kirkjugólf (church floor), with summer access to the awesome Lakagígar craters *(see pp38–9)*. The town's name – literally Church Farm Monastery – reflects its origins in 1186 as a convent. Moving west, Skaftafell in Vatnajökull National Park *(see pp18–19)* is not too far on the other side of the black, sandy spread of the Skeiðarársandur desert. *Map E5*

10 Jökulsárlón

An essential stop on the long journey between Vík and Höfn, Jökulsárlón's icebergs, glacier tongue and rushing waters – not to mention the bizarre sight of ice boulders on the beach – break the monotony of bleak expanses of black gravel along the coastal fringes. Seals and occasional orca (killer whales) are the pick of wildlife commonly encountered here, although there is plenty of birdlife too. Half-hour lagoon cruises are an option in summer *(see pp26–7)*. *Map G5*

Icebergs at Jökulsárlón

A Day in South Iceland

Morning

Begin a classic "Golden Circle" tour by heading northeast from Reykjavík up Route 36, looking out along the way for the boxy, two-storey white house of the late author and Nobel Laureate Halldór Laxness. After reaching Þingvallavatn's blue spread you arrive on the west side of the **Þingvellir** rift valley, where it is time to spend an hour – or the entire day – soaking up the events and landscapes at Iceland's cultural heart. Cross the rift and take Route 365 to **Laugarvatn**, where you could stop and have a swim at the National School for Sports, before pressing further along routes 37 and 35 to spectacular water features at **Geysir** and **Gullfoss**.

Afternoon

Have lunch at either Hótel Geysir – where you can get a proper three-course meal – or at Gullfoss' Visitor Centre, whose café does excellent lamb soup. Then follow Route 35 southwest to **Skálholt** *(see p66)*, a bishopric and educational centre since the 11th century. Route 35 continues southwest from Skálholt past the **Kerið** crater *(see p110)* to **Selfoss**, a busy town on the River Ölfusá, whose bridge was the cause of Iceland's first strike. The highway runs straight back to Reykjavík via the hot-house town of **Hveragerði** (famous for its flowers and vegetables), or you can detour coastwards to the villages of **Stokkseyri** and **Eyrarbakki** *(see p110)*.

Left **Skógar Museum** Right **Bridge between two continents, near Keflavík**

Best of the Rest

1 Mýrdalsjökull

This impressive south-coast icecap conceals the dangerous Katla volcano. The lowest glacier tongue, Sólheimajökull, is accessible off Route 1, where you can ice-climb, ride a snow-mobile or go dogsledding. *Map D6 • www.mountainguides.is; www.arcanum.is; www.dogsledding.is*

2 Kerið Crater

Beautiful, deep but small crater, north of Selfoss, best viewed on a sunny day to appreciate the red and black slopes contrasting with the blue water.

3 Skógar

Tiny community at the foot of Skógafoss *(see p33)*, with a hotel, hostel and campsite but little else apart from the Skógar Museum *(see p62)* and a superb hike to Þórsmörk *(see p57)*.

4 Hveragerði

Iceland's major hothouse town, using geothermal heat to grow flowers and vegetables on commercial scale. There is a horticultural college, hiking trails and a swimming pool. *Map C5*

5 Leirubakki

Farm and hotel on Mount Hekla, with a volcano museum and lava-block hot tub with views of the mountain, on the road to Landmannalaugar *(see pp24–5)*. *Map D5 • Route 26 • 487 8700 • Summer buses between Reykjavík and Landmannalaugar • www.leirubakki.is*

6 Hafnir Continental Bridge

The European and American continental plates separate most visibly at Þingvellir – the bridge allows you to cross between the continents. *Map C5*

7 Sudurnes Science and Learning Center

Very unusual museum full of microscopic sea creatures. Do not miss the stuffed walrus. *Map B5 • Garðvegur 1, 245 Sandgerði • 423 7551 • Adm • www.thekkingarsetur.is*

8 Hvolsvöllur Saga Centre

Lively exhibition of Viking-era re-creations. *Map C6 • Hlíðarvegur 14, Hvolsvöllur • 487 8781 • Open summer: 9am–6pm daily; winter: 10am–5pm Sat & Sun • Adm • www.njala.is*

9 Þórbergssetur

Museum dedicated to writer Þórbergur Þórðarson (1888–1974) is located in his home, also now a hotel. *Map G5 • Hali,781 Hornarfjörður • 478 1078 • Adm • www.thorbergssetur.is*

10 Stokkseyri and Eyrarbakki

Two delightful villages with a maritime heritage, old wooden houses, great seafood restaurants and the Húsið museum. *Map C5 • Húsið museum: www.husid.com*

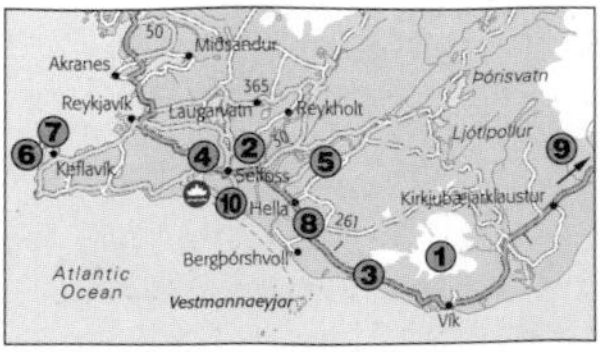

Price Categories

For a three course meal for one (without alcohol), with taxes and extra charges.	k	under ISK3,000
	kk	ISK3,000–5,000
	kkk	ISK5,000–7,000
	kkkk	ISK7,000–9,000
	kkkkk	over ISK9,000

Above **Exterior of Hótel Rangá, near Selfoss**

TOP 10 Places to Eat

1 Hótel Rangá

Nordic-European cuisine is served at this splendid restaurant in a rural hotel *(see p130)* with views of the finest salmon river in the country. Make sure you try the venison with wild mushrooms and berries. *kkkkk*

2 Menam

A great Thai place outside Reykjavík with all the favourites, from green curry to spicy prawn soup cooked absolutely fresh. No MSG used. *Map C5 • Eyravegur 8, Selfoss • 482 4099 • kk*

3 Hótel Geysir

Generous breakfast and lunch buffets and great views of the Geysir area, make this hotel restaurant the best place to eat in the area. *Map C5 • Haukadalur, Geysir • 480 6800 • kkkk*

4 Hótel Selfoss

Styled with a minimalist Nordic look, this up-market option is more comfortable than it appears, with a well-presented menu of Icelandic seafood and meat staples. Good place to impress a client. *Map C5 • Eyravegur 2, Selfoss • 480 2500 • kkkkk*

5 Gullfoss Kaffi

With wide vistas of the surrounding landscape – though not of Gullfoss itself – this spacious, wooden-framed café is a great spot to pull up for a bowl of lamb soup. *Map D4 • Gullfoss • 486 6500 • k*

6 Hótel Flúðir

Oddly aloof modern building on the edge of a farming town, Flúðir has splendid views and a menu featuring locally-grown hothouse vegetables and native meats. *Map C5 • Vesturbrún 1, Flúðir • 486 6630 • kkkk*

7 Rauða Húsið

A good reason to visit the charming Eyrarbakki village, this restaurant set in an old wooden house offers splendid lobster, lamb and fish dishes at a fraction of their cost in Reykjavik. *Map C5 • Búðarstíg 4, Eyrarbakki • 483 3330 • kkkk*

8 Hafið Bláa

Another good choice at the mouth of the Ölfusá river, where you should forget the other choices and just focus on their exceptional grilled lobster. *Map C5 • Þorlákshöfn, near Óseyrar Bridge, Eyrarbakki • 483 1000 • kkkk*

9 Kaffi Duus

Smart place not far from the Keflavík International Airport, so a good choice to tuck into lamb, lobster or salmon before heading homewards. *Map B5 • Duusgata 10, Keflavík • 421 7080 • kkk*

10 Hlíðarendi

A no-nonsense café inside Hvolsvöllur's main petrol station, but a handy pit-stop for tasty burgers, pizza and coffee after hiking in Þórsmörk. *Map C6 • Austurvegur 3, Hvolsvöllur • 487 8197 • k*

Left **Hot pool at Hveravellir** Right **Campsite at Landmannalaugar**

The Highland Interior

*I*NLAND FROM THE RELATIVELY FERTILE COASTLINE, *Iceland's Highland Interior is a beautiful wilderness of black gravel, lava plains and glaciated peaks, blasted by summer storms and severe winter frosts. Not surprisingly, the Interior has never been settled, but it remained crossed by the ghosts of numerous pack-horse trails used from Viking times until Route 1 around the country was completed in the 1970s. Open for just a few weeks in summer to 4WDs only, the most accessible of these routes are the Kjölur (from Gullfoss to near Akureyri) and Fjallabak (from Hella to Kirkjubæjarklaustur). Long-distance buses also follow these routes from June to September.*

TOP 10 Sights

1. The Kjölur Route
2. Hveravellir
3. Mount Hekla
4. Landmannalaugar
5. Veiðivötn & Langisjór
6. Þórsmörk Reserve
7. Lakagígar
8. Langjökull
9. Aldeyjarfoss
10. Herðubreið

View of the Langjökull glacier, from the Kjölur highway

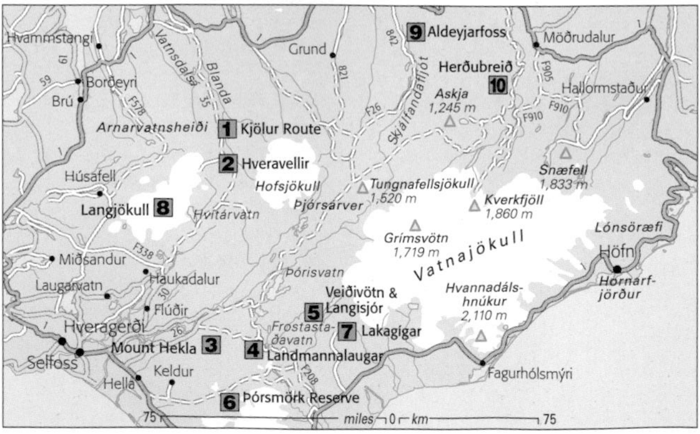

1 The Kjölur Route

The Kjölur Route (Kjalvegur) is the least difficult of the Highland roads, running for 170 km (106 miles) from Gullfoss *(see pp14–15)* to Route 1 near Blönduós *(see p93)*. All the major rivers have been bridged and the well-formed gravel track is safe. Sights along the way include Hveravellir's hot springs and the Langjökull icecap.
Map D4 • Bus times: www.bsi.is • Road open mid-Jun–late Aug • www.sterna.is

2 Hveravellir

Halfway along the Kjölur Route, Hveravellir is a desolate hot springs area with an outdoor hot tub, calcified mounds bubbling out boiling water, a strong smell of sulphur and a basic hut with bunkbeds run by the Icelandic Touring Club (www.fi.is). The 17th-century outlaw Eyvindur spent many winters here till local farmers chased him out. *Map D4*

3 Mount Hekla

East of Þjórsá river is Mount Hekla, which means "hooded," after the clouds that obscure its summit. It was once believed to be the entrance to hell, due to its eruptions followed by months of noisy "grumbling" (taken to be the sound of tormented souls). On a good day, you can see the mountain from Hella on Route 1, and you will pass close to it en route Landmannalaugar. Many companies run super-jeep circuits and trips to the mountain during summer. *Map D5*

Hikers on the Laugavegur trail

Þjórsá river, west of Mount Hekla

4 Landmannalaugar

Relatively accessible and just 3 or 4 hours from Reykjavík, Landmannalaugar delivers a full Highland experience. The road traverses volcanic wastelands, exciting river crossings, mountains and hot springs. There are enough hills, lava fields and lakes to explore for a day. You could even stay at the bunkhouse or the camp and spend 4 days hiking to Þórsmörk along the Laugavegur trail *(see p25)*. *Map D5*

5 Veiðivötn and Langisjór

Veiðivötn and Langisjór are part of a complex of inland waterways inside volcanic "stretch marks" southwest from Vatnajökull, reached off the F208 Fjallabak Route. There are some good fishing areas and unbelievably stark country. Veiðivötn is an area of tarns and streams while Langisjór is a narrow stretch of water. Both are accessible only along rough tracks and there is no public transport. *Map E5*

Highland Driving

Rough conditions, no settlements and nobody to help if something goes wrong all make it imperative that Highland roads are tackled only in high-clearance 4WD vehicles. Travel in convoy, check road conditions before setting out (www.vegagerdin.is) and give your route and estimated arrival time to someone reliable so rescue can be organized if needed.

6 Þórsmörk Reserve

Iceland's most popular hiking area, accessible only in a 4WD from the highway near Hvolsvöllur via the 30-km- (19-mile-) long F249 – though watch out for the potentially dangerous river crossing at the end – or by trekking in along Laugavegur or from Skógar via Fimmvörðuháls *(see p56)*. Set in an exceptionally pretty glacial valley, pick of the views at Þórsmörk are from Valahnúkur, an easy and short ascent, and the arduous and long Utigönguhöfði. There are plenty of self-catering cabins and campsites, and daily buses through the summer *(see p57)*. *Map D6*

7 Lakagígar

This 25-km- (16-mile-) long row of craters erupted with a vengeance in 1783, disrupting weather patterns all across Europe and nearly depopulating Iceland. Walking trails ranging between 20 minutes and 2 hours allow you to explore the line of cones and expansive lavafields, now partly buried under a thick matting of moss and heather. There is no accommodation on site, but mountain huts and campsites can be found along the road. Seasonal buses from Skaftafell National Park run here via Kirkjubæjarklaustur and the 60-km- (37-mile-) long F206 *(see p19)*. *Map E5 • Buses: Jun–4 Sep daily; schedule: www.bsi.is*

A cliff above Gullfoss

8 Langjökull

Iceland's second largest ice-cap, the "Long Glacier" west of the Kjölur Route feeds Hvítárvatn and Sandvatn lakes, which in turn drain into the Hvítá river on which the spectacular Gullfoss waterfalls are located *(see pp14–15)*. There is talk of damming another of its lakes, Hagavatn, for hydro power. Apart from seeing the glacier from the Kjölur or Kaldidalur routes, tours run up here for snowmobiling trips – you only get an hour but it is an exhilarating experience, like riding a jet ski on snow. *Map D4 • Year-round jeep tours from Reykjavík • www.adventures.is; www.glacierjeeps.is*

Eyjafjallajökull icecap from the summit of Valahnúkur

9 Aldeyjarfoss

Although these impressive falls on the Skjálfandafljót river sit

at the northern end of the otherwise difficult Sprengisandur Route, they are actually located on a good gravel road 30 km (19 miles) south of the Goðafoss waterfall *(see p33)*. Most vehicles can make it with care during the summer, but check conditions first. What makes Aldeyjarfoss so striking are the surrounding rock formations, where a layer of outlandishly fashioned basalt columns is capped by a thick blanket of solidified lava. Buses negotiating the Sprengisandur crossing between Reykjavík and Akureyri make it a point to stop here.
Map E3 • Bus schedule: www.re.is

Basalt columns at Aldeyjarfoss

10 Herðubreið

Known as the "Queen of the Mountains", Herðurbreið's spiky palagonite heights rise to an impressive 1,682 m (5,518 ft) northeast of Askja above the dismal Ódáðahraun ("Desert of Evil Deeds"). The slopes are laced by short freshwater springs, covered with pink blooms of arctic river beauty in July. You get good views on a clear day from the road to Kárahnjúkar *(p102)*, but if you fancy hiking, stop on the F88 between Mývatn and Askja *(see pp16–17)*. *Map F3*

A Drive Through the Highlands

Morning

Start early for this day trip to **Landmannalaugar** and bring a packed lunch. This will take upwards of 8 hours, depending on how many times you stop along the way. Head east along Route 1 from Reykjavík via Selfoss and Hella, then turn north up Route 264 to see the Viking buildings at **Keldur** farm. With **Hekla** looming behind, take a moment to appreciate Keldur's location – so close to an active volcano. Retrace the route towards Hella, then turn north along Route 268 for a half-hour run through lava fields to Hekla and the intersection with Route 26. You could turn left here to **Leirubakki** farm *(see p110)*, but for Landmannalaugar turn right, driving through the yellow pumice plain between Hekla and the Þjórsá river, before reaching the F225 junction, which heads east to Landmannalaugar. Pull up and enjoy your picnic lunch.

Afternoon

The F225 traverses the black sand wasteland of Hekla's northern foothills with several rivers before it reaches an intersection after 47 km (29 miles); turn right (south) down **Frostastaðavatn**'s lake-shore and then right again on to the 5-km- (3-mile-) long F224, which crosses a double fjord before reaching Landmannalaugar. Soak in the spring and then prepare to head back; once on Route 26 simply follow it south to the **Vegamót** road-house between Hella and Selfoss.

STREETSMART

Left **Tourist hut at Landmannalaugar** Right **Visitors on a puffin-viewing trip**

TOP 10 Planning Your Trip

1 Passports and Visas

Most visitors, including those from the UK and Ireland, Canada, the EU, USA, Australia, New Zealand and countries signed up to the Schengen Agreement, do not need a visa to enter Iceland for a visit under 90 days. You must have three months validity on your passport to enter the country. *www.utl.is*

2 Tourist Information

The main tourist information centre is in Reykjavík, offering information and brochures on accommodation, tours, dining, nightlife, money-saving cards and tax refunds. There are smaller offices at Keflavík airport and other towns.

3 Weather

Iceland's climate is temperate and milder than most people think. Temperature in summer can reach 23°C (74°F); winters are around 0°C (32°F). Autumn and spring are the wettest months. Snow is more common in the north than the south, which is warm and wet. *www.vedur.is*

4 When to Go

The midnight sun and summer temperatures make mid-June to mid-August the most popular time to visit. In the winter, lack of sunlight makes it less hospitable, and the interior is not accessible (many bus routes to this part do not begin until late June when the snow melts). You stand a good chance of seeing the aurora borealis from November to February. Spring and autumn have roughly balanced periods of day and night.

5 What to Pack

Bring a variety of warm, wind and waterproof clothes as the weather can be unpredictable. Sunscreen, sunglasses and a good quality eye mask are vital during the summer. Hikers need sturdy hiking boots. Don't forget your camera and your swimming gear for the hot springs.

6 Time Zone

Iceland follows the Greenwich Mean Time and is 5 hours ahead of US Eastern Standard Time. It does not observe Daylight Saving Time.

7 Currency

The island's currency is the Icelandic króna (ISK) or krónur in plural. Money can be exchanged on arrival. Foreign currency is accepted at Keflavík airport and some shops in Reykjavík. MasterCard and Visa are accepted but in rural areas, cash is useful.

8 Insurance

This is relatively a safe country but you are advised to take out travel and health insurance and check policy exclusions, especially if planning on hiking or adventure travel. Visitors from UK can take an EHIC health card, which covers basic national healthcare.

9 Current and Phone Adapters

Iceland has standard European electrical voltage and frequency (240V, 50Hz) so North American electrical devices will need converters. Plugs are two-pin and UK and North American items will need adapters. Most European mobile phones work on Iceland's GSM network but North American ones do not.

10 Special Equipment

Riding clothing and angling gear used outside Iceland must be disinfected, as per regulations, and certified by a vet before entry. If not, it will be disinfected at your cost. *www.customs.is*

Directory

Tourist Information Offices

Map K2 • Aðalstræti 2, 101 Reykjavík • 590 1550 • www.visitreykjavik.is

Map B5 • Keflavík airport • 425 6010 • www.reykjanes.is

Map E2 • Hafnarstræti 82, Akureyri • 462 3300 • www.nordurland.is

Preceding pages **Diners at Perlan's rooftop restaurant**

Left **Kirsuberjatréð gift shop, Reykjavík** Right **Tax refund booth, Reykjavík**

TOP 10 Useful Information

1 Useful Websites

The official tourist board website is www.visiticeland.com. Another good source of general information is www.icelandnaturally.com. The official Reykjavík website is www.visitreykjavik.is. Daily life and news on the island is covered on www.icelandreview.com. Foodies must visit www.icelandlocalfoodguide.is; hikers will like www.icelandtoday.is and www.nat.is, while www.angling.is for anglers. Weather information is at www.vedur.is. Younger visitors might like to visit www.grapevine.is to find out about nightlife; the selection of blogs on www.icelandexpress.com also provides a good flavour of the country.

2 Opening Hours

Office hours are Monday–Friday 9am–5pm, changing to 8am–4pm during June, July and August. Shops are open Monday–Friday 10am–6pm, Saturday from 10am until between 1 and 4pm. Some supermarkets are open until 11pm seven days a week. Banks are open Monday–Friday 9:15am–4pm. Outside Reykjavík, the hours may be shorter.

3 Public Holidays

Businesses, banks and most shops are closed on New Year's Day, Maundy Thursday, Good Friday, Easter Sunday, Easter Monday, First Day of Summer (usually third Thursday in April), Labour Day (May 1), Ascension Day, Whit Sunday, Whit Monday, National Day (June 17), Bank Holiday (First Monday in August), Christmas Eve (from noon), Christmas, December 26 and New Year's Eve (from noon).

4 Smoking Regulations

Smoking is prohibited in bars, restaurants, clubs and cafés across Iceland. There are no designated smoking areas inside and smoking outside is also restricted to some areas. You cannot smoke on public transport.

5 Embassies and Consulates

The foreign embassies in central Reykjavík include: USA: Laufásvegur 21, 595 2200, http://iceland.usembassy.gov; UK: Laufásvegur 31, 550 5100, www.gov.uk/government/world/iceland; Canada: Túngata 14, 575 6500, www.canada.is; France: Túngata 22, 551 7621, www.ambafrance-is.org; Germany: Laufásvegur 31, 530 1100, www.reykjavik.diplo.de; Japan: Laugavegur 182, 6th floor, 510 8600, japan@itn.is.

6 Tipping

There is no tipping in Iceland – service charge is included in all bills. It may even be considered an insult to tip. You might make an exception for fishing guides but otherwise it is standard to pay the bill and no more.

7 Sale Periods

There are no regular sale periods in Iceland – they are at the retailer's discretion. Midsummer and January tend to see shops reducing prices.

8 Tax and VAT Refunds

All prices include VAT, which on most goods is 25.5%. Tourists get a 15% tax-free refund on single items costing ISK 4,000 or more. Ask for a tax-free form when buying. There are refund booths at Keflavík airport, on Seyðisfjörður ferries, at Reykjavík tourist office and in Reykjavík malls.
www.iceland.is

9 Electricity and Weights and Measures

Electricity is standard European 240V, 50 Hz. Weights and measures are metric.

10 Language

Icelanders learn English from an early age and most speak it well, albeit with a charming and quirky accent. You are only likely to find a language barrier if you were to speak in Icelandic since Icelanders are not used to foreigners trying to speak their language and usually just reply in English.

The website www.grapevine.is carries local news about Reykjavík and ideas on going out.

Left **Leifur Eiríksson Terminal, Keflavík International Airport** Right **Cruise liner, Reykjavík harbour**

TOP 10 Getting to Iceland

1 By Air

It takes about 3 hours to reach Iceland by air from Europe and 5–6 hours from the USA. Icelandair flies into Keflavík airport, 50 km (31 miles) from Reykjavík, from the USA, Canada and Europe. Budget airline WOW Air flies into Keflavík from the UK and Europe.

2 Transport Security Regulations

Passengers can bring only a restricted quantity of liquids through security screening and in hand baggage. Each item may not exceed 100 ml (3.4 fl oz) of liquid and all containers must be carried in a 1-litre (34-fl oz) transparent plastic bag with a zip seal. Clearly labeled medication, baby food and foods for special diets may also be carried.

3 Duty Free Shopping

There is a duty free shop in the arrivals hall at Keflavík airport as well as in the departure lounge. Alcohol is significantly less expensive here than in the state-controlled alcohol shops in Iceland.

4 Leifur Eiríksson Terminal, Keflavík International Airport

The shops at Leifur Eiríksson Terminal offer a selection of international brands and exclusive local products, such as Blue Lagoon beauty treatments and Brennivín. There are also a number of bars and cafés. ⓢ *Map B5 • 235 Keflavikurflugvollur • 425 6000 • www.kefairport.is*

5 Reykjavík Domestic Air Terminal

This small airport in central Reykjavík serves Greenland, the Faroe Islands and the rest of Iceland. Air Iceland flies from here to Akureyri, the Westman Islands, Egilsstaðir, Vopnafjörður, Grímsey and Isafjörður. Eagle Air flies from here to Höfn, Sáuðárkrókur, Gjögur and Bíldudalur. Both run day tours of Iceland and Greenland. ⓢ *Map L6 • Reykjavík airport, 101 Reykjavík • 424 4000 • www.isavia.is*

6 Other Domestic Air Terminals

Iceland's other airports *(see above)* are very small and serve only domestic flights, with the exception of Akureyri, which has flights to Copenhagen in the summer with WOW Air and Egilsstaðir. They are mainly single runway airports with routes operated by Eagle Air or Air Iceland, with multiple daily flights to Reykjavík.

7 Cheap Flights

Icelandair and WOW Air regularly run sales on their websites. Sign up for email alerts from WOW Air for the very cheapest deals on offer. Skyscanner is a good way to compare prices for the cheapest deals. The cheapest way to reach Reykjavík from Keflavík airport is on the Flybus. ⓢ *www.icelandair.com; www.wow.is; www.skyscanner.net; www.flybus.is*

8 By Ferry

Smyril Line ferries sail from Denmark and the Faroe Islands to Seyðisfjörður weekly from April to October. It takes three nights from Denmark. You can take a car, camper van or motorbike. It is not a budget option. ⓢ *Yviri via Strond 1, Torshavn, Faroe Islands • 298 345900 • www.smyrilline.com*

9 By Cruise Ship

Plenty of cruise ships visit Iceland in summer, stopping at Reykjavík, Isafjörður, Akureyri and Seyðisfjörður. These include Princess Cruises, Holland America, P&O cruises, Hurtigruten, Fred Olsen Cruises, Cunard and Silversea. The itineraries include Spitsbergen, Greenland, Canada, north Europe and Arctic Circle. ⓢ *www.princess.com; www.hollandamerica.com; www.fredolsencruises.com; www.silversea.com*

10 Customs Allowances

Passengers above 18 can bring in 200 cigarettes or 250g of tobacco products and those above 20 may also bring one litre of spirits, a litre of wine or six litres of beer.

Left **A view from Perlan** Centre **Road sign** Right **Aircraft taking off from Isafjörður Airport**

TOP 10 Getting Around Iceland

1 By Car

Driving is an easy way to get around Iceland *(see p122)*. Be aware, however, that the roads are not perfect, especially outside metropolitan areas where they may not be sealed. Route 1 is the only motorway; it runs around the whole country for 1,300 km (808 miles). Some highland roads are closed in bad weather. *www.vegagerdin.is/english*

2 Hiring a Car

There are car hire offices in Keflavík airport, downtown Reykjavík, Seyðisfjörður, Akureyri airport and other major towns around Iceland. You need a full international driving license and drivers under 25 may require additional cover. A 4WD is advised for driving in the interior and during the rains or winter.

3 By Bus

There are numerous daily services around Iceland from the BSÍ bus station in central Reykjavík. It takes seven hours to reach Akureyri. As there is no train service in Iceland, buses are the only means of public transport around the country besides domestic flights. Most services run daily or twice a day on weekends. *Map L4* • *Vatnsmýrarvegi 10, 101 Reykjavík* • *580 5400* • *4:30am–midnight daily* • *www.bsi.is*

4 Taxis

Taxis in Iceland are metered and have uniform fares. There is no tipping. Look for ranks outside major hotels or call one. Many also offer sightseeing tours and taxis to the airport ply at a fixed rate: ISK 13,000 for 1–4 passengers, ISK 16,000 for 5–8 passengers.

5 Ferry

Ferries run to a number of important islands off the coast of Iceland. There are daily services to the Westman Islands from Landeyjahöfn in the south, taking about 30 minutes. In the north, to reach Grímsey or Hrísey, you can take a daily ferry, and there are various ferry tours around the Western Fjords.

6 Cycling

Icelanders might laugh at you, but cycling has become an increasingly popular pursuit, despite unsealed gravel roads and unkind weather. There are several bike hire shops in Reykjavík and Akureyri. You are only permitted to cycle on roads, not off road as it might damage vulnerable vegetation.

7 Walking and Hiking

Reykjavík is small enough to walk around easily in a day, especially if you are staying in the 101 area. Hiking is popular around the country, particularly on the Landmannalaugar trail through the centre of Iceland. Websites on hiking trails are www.nat.is and www.icelandtoday.is.

8 Maps

You can purchase maps of Iceland in all good map and travel shops; in Reykjavík, bookshops such as Eymundsson sell detailed hiking maps. Maps are also available via Icelandic online shops www.randburg.is and www.nordicstore.net. The tourist office can also provide maps. *www.visiticeland.com*

9 GPS

GPS is the preferred method of navigation in Iceland as much of the country is uninhabited. With extreme weather conditions and a lack of mobile phone coverage, the highlands and a few rural areas can be dangerous without it. Some car rentals also offer GPS rental for the duration of your trip.

10 Seasonal Considerations

Transport here is subject to seasonal variation. Summer bus routes (June–August) are more frequent and winter services can be much reduced. Many mountain roads open only from July to mid-September. Domestic flights often get cancelled in bad weather and ferries take longer if the sea is rough. *www.vedur.is*

The Blue Lagoon bus runs return journeys to the spa from Reykjavík; www.bustravel.is

Left **Gravel road** Centre **Petrol station, Ísafjörður** Right **Counters at domestic airport, Reykjavík**

Top 10 Driving Tips

1 Driver's License and Insurance

All European and US driving licenses are valid in Iceland; UK visitors require both parts of their license. Visitors from other countries should check with their local motoring organizations. European drivers who bring their own vehicles do not need a Green Card or proof of third party insurance.

2 Car Rental Agencies

Downtown Reykjavík, Keflavík airport and Akureyri have many international and local car rental agencies; WOW Air and Icelandair offer fly-drive packages including car hire. The minimum age for hiring a car is 20 and 25 for jeeps. Hire cars may not be insured for highland driving.

3 Fuel

Fuel is priced by the litre. Self-service pumps are cheaper than attended ones; Atlantsolia and ÓB are the cheapest brands. Fill up when you can in rural areas. Most filling stations are open till 11:30pm. Those in Reykjavík and large towns often have automatic payment after closing time, accepting Visa credit cards and notes.

4 Speed Limits and Laws

The speed limit is 50 kmph (30 mph) unless otherwise marked. It is 80 kmph (50 mph) on gravel roads, 90 kmph (56 mph) on asphalt and 30 kmph (19 mph) in residential areas. Drivers and passengers must wear seat belts and headlights must be on at all times. Driving is on the right. It is against the law to drive after drinking alcohol.

5 Parking

Some Icelanders do not parallel park and might leave vehicles at strange angles anywhere along the street. Laws advise parking in the direction of traffic, 16 ft (5 m) from pedestrian crossings and intersections. Parking restrictions are clearly marked. Reykjavík and Akureyri have inexpensive multi-storey car parks.

6 Hazards

Roundabouts can be tricky. The inner lane has right of way over the outer; take the outer lane if planning to exit at the next junction. Be cautious when driving past schools and pedestrian crossings. Icelandic drivers do not habitually stop for pedestrians, who are frequently none too cautious in crossing roads.

7 Traffic Signals

Traffic lights follow European convention, with amber for caution, red for stop, red and amber together for stop but prepare to go, and green for go. The word *blindhæð* warns drivers of a blind hill, which can occur on single track roads and demands cautious driving.

8 Gravel Roads

Many of Iceland's rural roads are gravel, narrow and not suited to fast driving. Speed limits are reduced from 90 kmph (56 mph) to 80 kmph (50 mph) on these roads. Drive considerately and use passing places when you meet oncoming traffic. Take care especially where gravel roads meet asphalt and vice versa.

9 Driving in the Highlands

Driving off marked roads is prohibited as it can damage the land and you may be sued for compensation. Many rivers in highland areas are unbridged, so ensure conditions are safe before crossing. Mountain tracks are closed in winter and reopen in early July. Most require a 4WD. Always take a detailed map and GPS.

10 Livestock and Wildlife

There is a lot of unfenced territory in Iceland and it is common to find sheep, horses or cows on roads all over the country. This can be dangerous. Drive carefully as you may be liable to compensation claims if you cause injury or death.

In Iceland, vehicle headlights have to be on at all times, day and night.

Left **Whale-watching trip, off Húsavík** Right **Gravel road to Hekla**

TOP 10 Things to Avoid

1 Pub-Crawling on Payday

Traditionally payday is the day to splash your cash in town on a pub crawl. After the global market crash, the party spirit has diminished, but you can still expect a procession of cars around the city on Friday and Saturday nights, long queues at the bar and a little late-night brawling.

2 Fishing Without a Permit

You need a permit to fish in Iceland and will be subject to hefty fines if you do not have one. Fishing season runs June to September and there are restrictions on the length of the fishing season on most rivers. You may not fish for longer than 12 hours a day. Rule violations are taken very seriously.

3 Solo Wilderness Driving

Iceland's habitat can take years to recover from damage, so off-road and solo wilderness driving is frowned upon. Mobile phone coverage in the highlands is not reliable and roads are rarely used. If your vehicle has broken down, stay with it. Always take a map and a GPS device.

4 Speeding on Gravel Roads

The majority of road accidents in Iceland happen where paved roads change to gravel. Gravel roads are common in rural areas and subject to a speed limit *(see p122)*. Drivers should reduce speed before the changeover to gravel to keep control. Loose gravel on road shoulders also causes accidents.

5 Rush Hour in Reykjavík

From 7:45–9am and 4–6:30pm, traffic in Reykjavík can be taxing. Avoid travelling at this time if at all possible; the city's narrow roads are frequently gridlocked. It isn't a big city, but most people have a car and public transport is under-used at the moment.

6 Buying Sealskin

Be careful what you buy in Iceland. Fish skin gloves, wallets and belts are fine, but if you buy anything made of seal-skin and try to take it back, US customs will confiscate it. There are no such restrictions by the UK or European customs departments.

7 Currency Exchange

Since the Icelandic banking crisis in 2008 the value of the Icelandic krona has dropped. Although clear signs of a recovery are starting to show, it is still advisable not to change money anywhere other than at major banks, hotels or bureaux de change.

8 Recreational Drugs and Homebrew

Penalties for possession, use and trafficking of drugs are severe, with huge fines and custodial sentences imposed. Alcohol is sold through state-controlled shops (Vínbúðin) and is highly taxed. Homebrew – often called moonshine (*landi* in Icelandic) – is illegal and can be lethal. It can cause blindness and even death, so it is simply not worth the risk and should be avoided.

9 Sailing in Bad Weather

Ferries will cancel their services in dangerous conditions, but such are the conditions in the north Atlantic that even fair weather sailings can be very uncomfortable for the casual traveller. Seasickness is very common, even on whale-watching cruises, let alone longer crossings. Most ferries carry travel sickness remedies.

10 Pickpockets and Bag Snatchers

Crime is rare, but you would be advised to take special care in busy bars and clubs late at night in Reykjavík and around the Hlemmur local bus centre. Keep an extra eye on your belongings and valuables in crowds, on public transport and while queuing at busy tourist attractions.

Left **Main post office, Reykjavík** Centre **Iceland bank sign** Right **Grapevine newspaper**

TOP 10 Banking and Communications

1 Banking Hours
Banks are open Monday to Friday 9:15am–4pm. Outside Reykjavík, the hours may be shorter. There are several banks in downtown Reykjavík, Keflavík airport, Akureyri and in all large towns. Outside major towns you will find ATMs in larger stores, malls and at petrol stations.

2 Currency Exchange
Banks post legal exchange rates in their branches; you can also use credit and debit cards to withdraw krónur from ATMs, but be aware that some bank cards charge extra for currency exchange. Check before travel.

3 Traveller's Cheques
Traveller's cheques may be used in Iceland but it is nearly a cashless economy, so credit and debit cards are more useful. You can change traveller's cheques at banks, hotels and post offices; pounds sterling, dollars and euros are the recommended currencies. There is no limit to the amount you can bring into the country.

4 ATMs
ATMs are common. In metropolitan areas they are found outside banks, in larger stores and at some petrol stations. Check with your bank before travel to see if you can use your card abroad and what surcharge will be levied. Cash is useful in more remote rural areas.

5 Credit Cards
Credit cards are widely accepted. Visa and MasterCard are the main brands used, along with Visa debit cards. American Express is not accepted in some places. Cards are commonly used but some establishments do not allow card use for purchases totalling less than ISK 500.

6 Post Offices
Post offices are found in most major towns and are open from Monday to Friday only, from 9am–4 or 6pm, depending on the size of the town. Look out for the post horn logo on a red mailbox. International post to Europe takes 3 to 5 days and longer to other areas, while parcels are good value. Stamps are sold at hotels, bookshops and supermarkets throughout Iceland. *Map L2*
• Reykjavík central post office: Íslandspóstur, Pósthússtræti 5, 101 Reykjavík • 580 1200 • www.postur.is

7 Internet Access
Iceland has one of the world's highest Internet usage. Wi-Fi is available in many cafés and bookshops. The Reykjavík tourist information centre has Internet access (free for Reykjavík card holders) and it is available in many hotels and youth hostels. There are a number of Internet cafés in downtown Reykjavík around Austurvöllur.

8 Telephones
Note that in the Icelandic phonebook, people are listed in order of first name, not surname. The mobile phone network is reliable along Iceland's coastline but not in the centre of the country. It is a GSM system, compatible with European networks but not US ones. You can rent cell phones. The country code is 354.

9 Newspapers
Morgunblaðið, *Fréttablaðið* and *DV* are the three main newspapers on sale in Iceland, published in Icelandic. You can get English newspapers and magazines in various hotels and bookshops. *Iceland Review* is a quality monthly English-speaking lifestyle and news magazine worth picking up. Free newspaper *Grapevine* is a good what's-on guide.

10 Television
There are three main TV channels in Iceland and much of the content is in English and subtitled. Many hotels have satellite TV and screen major sporting events such as international and Premiership football.

Left **Hot pool, Hveravellir** Right **A 4WD crossing a stream in the Highlands**

TOP 10 Security and Health

1 Security Tips

Iceland is a safe country to travel in but the usual advice applies. Always lock your car, don't leave valuables on display and don't flash your cash. Keep an eye on your belongings in crowded areas.

2 Crime

The island has one of the lowest crime rates in the world. However, minor assaults, petty burglary and drug-related crimes do occur, primarily in Reykjavík. The country has a strict gun law.

3 Police

Iceland's police officers, *lögreglan,* wear black uniforms and police cars are white with blue lettering and blue and red stripes. They carry pepper spray and extendable batons but, with the exception of airport police, no firearms. *Map M3 • Main police station: Hverfisgata 113 • 444 1000*

4 Emergency Phone Numbers

The 24-hour emergency services number for fire, ambulance and police is 112. All calls are free of charge. For emergency doctors on call, dial 1770. This links to a medical centre in Kópavogur, a suburb of Reykjavík, for telephone advice, home visits or admissions. For dental emergencies, dial 575 0505.

5 Crossing Streams

Crossing unbridged streams in the countryside is an art. Never cross a stream in flood and never try to cross just above a waterfall. Use a hiking stick to gauge the depth; anything thigh high or deeper is dangerous. Do not cross a stream by car that you do not think you can walk across.

6 Coastal Hazards

The coastline and beaches in Iceland are not typically guarded. Beware of incoming tides and estuaries when walking and take local advice. Make sure someone knows where you are. In areas such as the caves at Reynishverfi near Vík, walkers are vulnerable to incoming tides and rockslides, so be careful. *Icelandic Coastguard • 545 2000 • www.lhg.is*

7 Sun Care

The sun here is very strong. Do not be fooled by the name! Bring sunglasses, sun cream and a hat, especially if you are walking or planning to spend time outdoors. Windburn is also common and you might want to pack aftersun too – it is expensive in Iceland.

8 Avalanches, Landslides and Mudslides

Avalanches, landslides and mudslides have claimed many lives in Iceland over the years. Check the meteorological advice if you are planning to go walking in vulnerable areas such as the Western Fjords, especially during springtime. Avalanche warnings are posted online. Heavy rains can lead to mudslides year-round, so check the weather forecast. *Recorded weather forecast (in English): 902 0600 • For weather updates check: www.vedur.is*

9 Healthcare and Prescriptions

You are advised to bring all medications you might need with you. All EU citizens holding an EHIC card are eligible for the same level of state healthcare as they receive at home but US and other citizens have to pay. Prescription prices vary and ambulances incur a non-refundable cost. Pharmacies *(apótek)* are often open until late.

10 Water Quality and Swimming

The water is potable here. Public swimming pools, *sundlaug*, are geothermally heated to a constant temperature of 28°C (83°F). The water is very clean – but not chemically cleaned – and you are required to wash before entering. When bathing in natural pools, check the temperature as it can vary due to seismic shifts and you can get burned.

Above **Perlan dome, Reykjavík**

Top 10 Budget Tips

1 Online Discounts

Check prices online before buying tickets. From Europe, Skyscanner shows the cheapest day of each month, and the cheapest months to fly with WOW Air, who also have regular offers. Icelandair has discounts for short periods advertised on their website. The same applies to Icelandair Hotels and many international chains. *www.skyscanner.net • www.wowiceland.co.uk • www.icelandair.com • www.icelandairhotels.com*

2 Travel Outside Peak Season

The peak season in Iceland is June to August. If you can be flexible with dates, you will find that travel outside these months is much cheaper, with the exception of mid-October in Reykjavík, when the Iceland Airwaves music festival pushes up flight and accommodation rates.

3 The Reykjavík Welcome Card

If you are visiting Reykjavík, make the most of this discount card. It can be bought at the Tourist Information Centre and a number of other locations. It gives you free admission to the thermal pools and museums, unlimited bus travel, free Internet access and other reductions. *www.visitreykjavik.is*

4 Free Attractions

There are plenty of free things to do in Reykjavík. Visit Perlan (the Pearl); take a free walking tour from the tourist office; visit Hallgrímskirkja; or walk down to the beach where the thermal pool is free. There are plenty of free cultural events throughout the year, as well as some lively free festivals. *www.freecitytravel.com*

5 Transport Tips

Taxis from the airport are significantly more expensive than the airport shuttle. Going via the Blue Lagoon on the way to or from the airport is another way to save money, with Flybus/Reykjavík Excursions from the BSÍ bus station. *www.flybus.is*

6 Cheap Stays

Bring a sleeping bag if you want to save money in the summer – many guesthouses have "sleeping bag" places that are cheaper than fully made-up beds. The country's youth hostels are top-notch – you can book private rooms in Reykjavík, and you might have others all to yourself. Or bring a tent. *575 6700 • info@hostel.is • www.hostel.is*

7 Eating Out

Tasty soups in the mid-range or rural restaurants are good value as you usually get free refills. The same goes for coffee. Many restaurants offer children's portions. In bars, local beer is cheaper than imported beer and many have happy hours. You can save money by not buying bottled water as the tap water is quite good.

8 Shopping

Buy local goods as Iceland imports so much from overseas that you won't find bargains on items available back home. If you want to buy Icelandic gifts or oddities, the majority are available cheaper at the airport duty-free store. Don't forget to claim tax refunds for items over ISK 4,000.

9 Fishing Discounts

Fishing isn't cheap, particularly if you are caught contravening any of the strict rules. You can buy an Angler's Card which allows access to around 36 sites for trout, charr and salmon fishing. Check conditions and timing with the tourist office – the fishing season doesn't run all year round. *www.nat.is*

10 Travel Insurance

Check your travel insurance policy carefully beforehand, particularly any exceptions to your policy. The unpredictable weather and adventure sports can cause surprise mishaps. European visitors should carry the EHIC card for any emergency.

Left **Fish Market restaurant, Reykjavík** Right **Campsite at Fjallabak Nature Reserve**

TOP 10 Accommodation and Dining Tips

1 Book Early
Book hotels well ahead, particularly during the summer, as popular locations such as Mývatn book up early. Hotels in Iceland's smaller towns and popular domestic holiday spots can fill up quickly, especially if there is an event in town. With often limited accommodation options, it pays to plan ahead.

2 Shoulder Seasons
Outside the main summer season, prices drop considerably. The shoulder seasons of autumn (September–October) and spring (April–May) bring great savings on hotel rates. Christmas and New Year are usually very pricey. Both these periods can be rainy; weather-wise, late May and early September are great times to visit on a budget.

3 Package Deals
WOW Air and Icelandair offer attractive package deals with their flights, often including good hotels at bargain rates plus car hire and tours. Online consolidators such as Lastminute and Opodo also have package deals. Discover The World is the top class package tour operator to Iceland. ✆ *www.icelandair.com • www.wowiceland.co.uk • www.lastminute.com • www.opodo.com • www.discover-the-world.co.uk*

4 Self-Catering
Groups and families might find that renting self-catering apartments or units with kitchenettes will help their budgets, although be aware that all food is expensive in Iceland. Youth hostels also offer shared kitchens. Farm stays are a popular choice with families, although you will need to hire a car.

5 Mountain Huts
Backpackers and walkers can stay in mountain or wilderness huts on established walking trails such as the Landmannalaugar–Þórsmörk forest walk. Book at least a month in advance, via either of the two main hiking organizations. The alternative, camping in strong winds and horizontal rain, is not much fun. ✆ *The Iceland Touring Association: www.fi.is • Útivist: www.utivist.is*

6 Daily Specials
The cheapest or best value menu in an Icelandic restaurant is usually on the daily specials board or a fixed menu. Local and seasonal food is naturally the best value in any case: think lamb, salmon and seafood. Avoid tourist trap eateries advertising puffin suppers for the best prices.

7 Fish at Discounts
Seafood dishes tend to be cheaper than the meat dishes in most restaurants, and what's more, the country's fish, fresh from the North Atlantic, has a fantastic reputation. Try cod, haddock, halibut, ray, redfish, herring or lobster. For a quirky snack, *harðfiskur* (dried cod) is available in most corner shops.

8 Water
In restaurants, there is no need to order bottled mineral water unless you want sparkling water. Tap water is of the same quality as mineral water. If you are walking in Iceland, take a bottle with you and fill up at no cost from the tap or from running streams.

9 Wine and Beer
House wines bought by the half-bottle or carafe might work out as better value than wine by the glass. Iceland imports all its wine bar one brand, Kvöldsól – made from blueberries, crowberries and rhubarb in Húsavík. The cheapest beer brands are the widely available locally-brewed Viking Gold and Thule Beer.

10 Cultural Centres
Iceland's museums and cultural centres often have bargain-priced eateries for lunch and coffee breaks – no entry fee required. These include: Reykjavík City Hall, Hveragerði greenhouse centre and Kjarvalstaðir art gallery in Reykjavík.

Visit www.icelandlocalfoodguide.is for the best of Iceland's food and drink.

Left **Interior of Hótel Plaza** Right **Façade of Hótel Reykjavík Centrum**

Top 10 Hotels in Reykjavík City Centre

1 Reykjavík 101

Close to the capital's main shopping street and National Opera House, this smart place is stark on the outside. Inside, the modern, bright rooms have a contemporary minimalist look complete with wooden flooring, large beds and marble bathrooms. Amenities include a gym and spa. *Map L2 • Hverfisgata 10 • 580 0101 • www.101hotel.is • kkkkk*

2 Hótel Holt

Holt's façade has the appeal of 1980s carpark architecture, but once through the doors you are in one of the most plush old-style venues in town. It is wood panelled and has its own collection of 19th-century Icelandic artworks and an outstanding restaurant. *Map L3 • Bergstaðastræti 37 • 552 5700 • www.hotelholt.is • kkkk*

3 Hótel Borg

Wonderful Art Deco building whose elegance and style is reflected in the immaculate rooms, complete with genuine period furnishings. The decor is black and white and floors are marble. *Map L2 • Pósthússtræti 11 • 551 1440 • www.hotelborg.is • kkkkk*

4 Hótel Reykjavík Centrum

A modern hotel in an old building on an ancient site: the timber and red corrugated iron exterior sits above the remains of a 7th-century Viking settlement. Rooms retain their century-old feel but are tastefully modernized. Good service and a renowned restaurant. *Map K2 • Aðalstræti 16 • 514 6000 • www.hotelcentrum.is • kkkkk*

5 Hótel Plaza

Light, airy modern building with rooms to match; timber flooring, white walls and furnishings, and the suites have views of the older part of the city. A host of good restaurants nearby. *Map K2 • Aðalstræti 4 • 595 8500 • www.plaza.is • kkkk*

6 Hótel Frón

Ninety *en suite* rooms and self-service apartments with kitchenettes, and the usual services plus Wi-Fi. The efficient, modern Nordic look elsewhere doesn't prepare you for the Mexican-cantina-style bistro and bar. Nice terrace café, too. *Map M3 • Laugarvegur 22A • 511 4666 • www.hotelfron.is • kkk*

7 Hótel Klöpp

Streamlined place with small rooms and open-plan bathrooms; it is friendly, efficient and located just off bustling Laugarvegur. A sound option for a short stay. Rooms on the upper floors are quieter and some have nice views of the sea. *Map M2 • Klapparstígur 26 • 595 8500 • www.centerhotels.com • kkk*

8 Hótel Óðinsvé

Excellent value family-owned place that manages to balance the homey 1930s building with modern minimalist chic. Its location off the main streets means less likelihood of being disturbed by rowdy weekend merrymakers. A good restaurant specializing in grills. *Map L3 • Þórsgata 1 • 511 6200 • www.hotelodinsve.is • kkk*

9 Hótel Leifur Eiríksson

Across the magnificent Hallgrímskirkja, this small boutique hotel has great views of the church and nearby streets from its upper rooms. You don't get a huge amount of space, but rooms are tidy and it is unquestionably value for money. *Map M3 • Skólavörðustíg 45 • 562 0800 • www.hotelleifur.is • kk*

10 Fosshotel Lind

Reliable hotel with comfortable, barrack-like facilities and helpful staff. There is nothing lacking in the services offered, but the rooms are on the small side and could do with some more features. However, good for a brief stay. *Map N3 • Rauðarástígur 18 • 562 3350 • www.fosshotel.is • kkk*

Lobby bar of the Radisson Blu Saga Hótel

Price Categories

For a standard double room per night (with breakfast if included), taxes and extra charges.	**k**	under ISK10,000
	kk	ISK10,000–20,000
	kkk	ISK20,000–30,000
	kkkk	ISK30,000–40,000
	kkkkk	over ISK40,000

Top 10 Hotels Around Reykjavík

1 Radisson Blu Saga Hótel

Located close to the city centre, this business and conference venue enjoys views of Rekjavík from all rooms. Master suites are very stylish, with dark wooden floors. All guests have access to the health centre. *Map J3 • Hagatorg, 107 Reykjavík • 525 9900 • www.radissonblu.com • kkkk*

2 Hilton Reykjavík Nordica

As the name suggests, the decor here is distinctly biased towards monochromatic furnishings and pine flooring. In-room safe, blackout curtains (for the luminous summer nights) and bathroom phones are a nice touch. *Map Q4 • Suðurlandsbraut 2, 108 Reykjavík • 444 5000 • www.hiltonreykjavik.com • kkkkk*

3 Grand Hótel Reykjavík

Iceland's largest hotel in an impressive tower block, it has a competent restaurant and a huge spa and fitness centre. Conference rooms make it an ideal business venue. *Map Q3 • Sigtún 38, 105 Reykjavík • 514 8000 • www.grand.is • kkkkk*

4 Hótel Park Inn Ísland

Large hotel which uses coloured furnishings, breaking away from the spartan palates usually associated with Icelandic accommodation. Its location, close to the Botanical Gardens and free access to Reykjavík's swimming pools, is a bonus. *Map R4 • Ármúli 9, 108 Reykjavík • 595 7000 • www.parkinn.com • kkk*

5 Hótel Cabin

Tidy budget hotel with basic but clean furnishings and relatively compact rooms. Upper floors have ocean views, while some rooms are designed with inward-facing windows for relief during the bright summer nights. Great-value lunch buffet at the restaurant. *Map N3 • Borgartún 32, 105 Reykjavík • 511 6030 • www.hotelcabin.is • kk*

6 Hótel Björk

A drab exterior but the good-sized rooms with views, friendly staff, decent restaurant and location make this option a firm favourite. *Map N3 • Brautarholt 22-24, 105 Reykjavík • 511 3777 • www.bjorkhotelreykjavik.com • kkkk*

7 Youth Hostel Rejkjavík

One of the few Icelandic youth hostels with private rooms as well as dormitories, which, along with its location near the Botanical Gardens and Laugardalur swimming pool, make it the best budget option in town. Advance booking is essential. *Map R3 • Sundlaugarvegur 34, 105 Reykjavík • 553 8110 • www.hostel.is • kk*

8 Hótel Laxnes

Low-set hotel in a semi-rural location near the former home of novelist Halldór Laxness. Double rooms and apartments with kitchenettes are good, but single rooms echo and are lonely. There is a golf course and pool nearby, with regular shuttle buses into town. *Map Q5 • Háholt 7, 270 Mosfellsbær • 566 8822 • www.hotellaxnes.is • kk*

9 Viking Village

Whole complex built around a Viking theme, with accommodation, restaurants, museum and stage shows. The hotel's exterior is a bit like a warehouse, but the rooms are surprisingly good, with the usual white paint and wooden floors. *Map P6 • Strandgata 55, 220 Hafnarfjörður • 565 1213 • www.fjorukrain.is • kk*

10 Hótel Örkin

Small budget hotel with few frills, run by the Faroese Seamen's Mission. It is well-cared for and with a friendly atmosphere. Church services are held on Sundays. Price includes breakfast but otherwise you will have to eat out. *Map P4 • Brautarholt 29, 105 Reykjavík • 568 0777 • www.hotelorkin.is • kkk*

Left **Interior of Hótel Búðir, Snæfellsnes Peninsula** Right **Hótel Framtíð, Djúpivogur**

TOP 10 Hotels Around Iceland

1 Hótel Rangá
Spendid countryside retreat with four-star comforts, especially worthwhile if salmon fishing on the nearby Rangá river appeals. Lodge-style pine cabins and main buildings, excellent restaurant and close to all south Iceland's attractions. *Map C5 • Hótel Rangá, Ringroad, near Hella • 487 5700 • www.hotelranga.is • kkkk*

2 Hótel Búðir
Soulful, atmospheric seaside setting, with only a dark wooden church and the nearby white cone of Snæfellsjökull for company. This refurbished old-style hotel is one of Iceland's romantic gems. Spoil yourself at the restaurant. *Map A4 • Hótel Búðir, 365 Snæfellsnes • 435 6700 • www.budir.is • kkk*

3 Fosshotel Skaftafell
You cannot help but feel that a lot more could have been done with the amazing glacier views, only visible from a few of the rooms. Otherwise a perfectly comfortable base for hiking at nearby Skaftafell National Park (closed in December). *Map F5 • Freysnes, 785 Öræfi • 478 1945 • www.fosshotel.is • kkk*

4 Hótel Klaustur
Strange to find such a large hotel in such a tiny place, though it is well placed for summer excursions to Skaftafell National Park and the Lakagígar craters. Has a decent restaurant and a small geothermal pool next door. *Map E5 • Klausturvegur 6, 880 Kirkjubæyjarklaustur • 444 4000 • www.icelandairhotels.com • kkk*

5 Hótel Hamar
Long, low hotel with outdoor hot tubs, top-notch restaurant and an excellent 18-hole golf course. Each room has a large window and door opening directly on to the grounds. Do not miss a visit to the Borgarnes Settlement Centre. *Map B4 • Golfvöllurinn Hamar, 310 Borgarnes • 433 6600 • www.icelandairhotels.com • kkk*

6 Hótel Hérað
The institution-like exterior should not deter you as the large rooms are tastefully furnished. The conference facilities are good and helpful staff is a bonus. Restaurant is fine but Café Nielsen up the road is better value. *Map G3 • Miðvangur 5-7, 700 Egilsstaðir • 471 1500 • www.icelandairhotels.com • kkk*

7 Hótel Gígur
This well-managed, modern hotel on Mývatn's southern shore has amazing views of the lake from the dining room. The rooms are a bit small for the price. Watch out for the summer flies outside the lobby. *Map F2 • Skútustaðir, 600 Mývatn • 464 4455 • www.keahotels.is • kkk*

8 Hótel KEA
The flagship of this small north Iceland chain is located in a grand old building in Akureyri. The rooms are well-furnished and quite spacious. The generous buffet breakfast gets a thumbs up. *Map E2 • Hafnarstræti 87–89, 600 Akureyri • 460 2000 • www.keahotels.is • kkkk*

9 Hótel Ísafjörður
The solid exterior, providing protection against severe winter storms, hides a warm, comfortable and friendly hotel whose staff go out of their way to help. Rooms are not huge, but have everything you will need for a night or two. Expensive but good restaurant. *Map B2 • Silfurtorg 2, 400 Ísafjörður • 456 4111 • www.hotelisafjordur.is • kkk*

10 Hótel Framtíð
This delightful old building overlooks Djúpivogur's attractive village harbour and is a good place to rest after a trip to Papey island. Rooms in the main hotel are modern and cosy; also hires out more ordinary wooden cabins and runs a campsite. *Map G4 • Vogaland 4, 765 Djúpivogur • 478 8887 • www.simnet.is/framtid • kkk*

Price Categories

For a standard double room per night (with breakfast if included), taxes and extra charges.

k	under ISK10,000
kk	ISK10,000–20,000
kkk	ISK20,000–30,000
kkkk	ISK30,000–40,000
kkkkk	over ISK40,000

Above **Gistiheimilið Sunna, Reykjavík**

Top 10 Guesthouses

1 Gistiheimilið Baldursbrá

In a residential area close to the bus terminal, this hospitable, cosy place provides spacious rooms with shared bathrooms and family-sized apartments, an outdoor hot tub, barbecue and sauna. Large breakfast buffet included in the price. *Map L4 • Laufásvegur 41, 101 Reykjavík • 552 6646 • baldursbra@centrum.is • kk*

2 Guesthouse Anna

Large rooms in a beautiful, comfortable house, fantastic food and a welcoming host. Rooms are *en suite* or with shared bathrooms. It is well-located in a quiet street close to the bus station. *Map L4 • Smáragötu 16, 101 Reykjavík • 562 1618 • www.guesthouseanna.is • kkk*

3 Gistiheimilið Sunna

Smart, hostel-like place close to Hallgrímskirkja. All rooms are clean and functional with access to a kitchenette, and there are either shared or private bathrooms. As is often the case in this late-partying city, noise can be a problem. *Map M3 • Þórsgata 26, 101 Reykjavík • 511 5570 • www.sunna.is • kkk*

4 Lava Hostel

This simple, self-catering guesthouse has 2–6 person rooms, shared bathrooms and full kitchen facilities. There is also a dormitory with sleeping-bag accommodation (bring your own or rent linen on-site). Buses to Reykjavík and the international airport stop nearby. *Map B5 • Hjallabraut 51, 220 Hafnarfjörður • 565 0900 • www.lavahostel.is • kk*

5 Gistiheimilið Egilsstöðum

More of a character hotel than a guesthouse, but still with a family-run atmosphere, set in a large renovated farmhouse just outside of town with grand views over the lake. Rooms are all *en suite*; there is a great restaurant here, too. *Map G3 • Off Route 1, Egilsstaðir • 471 1114 • www.egilsstadir.com • kkk*

6 Sólheimar Eco-Village

A stay in this sustainable community, founded in 1930, is an unforgettable experience that could change your life. As well as the comfy guesthouse, there are crafts workshops, a vegetarian restaurant, a sculpture garden and much more. *Map C5 • Grímsnes, 801 Selfoss • 480 4400 • www.solheimar.is • kk*

7 Skálholtsskóli

This accommodation is attached to the cathedral school at historic Skálholt. Summer concerts at the cathedral (www.sumartonleikar.is) are a bonus. Book in advance. *Map C5 • Skálholt • 486 8870 • www.skalholt.is • kk*

8 Gistiheimilið Geysir

Next to the geothermal springs area and a golf course, this self-catering guesthouse has single, double and triple rooms with a large kitchen. Most suited to groups, but can accommodate individual guests; book in advance. *Map C5 • Geysir • 486 8733 • www.geysirgolf.is • kk*

9 Gistiheimilið Hamar

Seasonal budget wing of Hótel Þórshamar, which also runs another guesthouse and a youth hostel. This modern block near the harbour has comfortable rooms; breakfast is available at the main hotel, which also has a spa, a sauna and hot tubs. *Map C6 • Herjólfsgata 4, Heimaey, Vestmannaeyjar • 481 2900 • May–Sep • www.hotelvestmannaeyjar.is • kk*

10 Gistiheimilið Hof

Long, turf-roofed building in a rural location with a sandy beach and romantic seascapes. The guesthouse has 6 self-contained units, with 3 double bedrooms, a bathroom, kitchenette and outdoor hot tub. *Map A4 • Hofgarðar, 365 Snæfellsbær • 435 6802 • www.gistihof.is • kkk*

Left **Hótel Aldan, Seyðisfjörður** Right **Edda Hótel, Vík**

TOP 10 Summer Hotels and Eddas

1 Hótel Aldan

Century-old wooden building by the harbour – once a bank – now converted into a 9 bed-room hotel with period furnishings, a bar and an excellent restaurant. More rooms are available in their nearby sister operation, Hótel Snæfell. *Map H3 • Norðurgata 2, 710 Seyðisfjörður • 472 1277 • www.simnet.is/aldanhf • kkk*

2 Hótel Stórutjarnir

Conveniently located between Akureyri and Mývatn, this modern lake-side hotel sits in a short, tight valley frequented by geese in summers. Facilities include *en suite* doubles, dormitories, a restaurant and attached thermal pool. *Map E2 • Stórutjarnir, Route 1 • 444 4890 • Jun–Aug • www.hoteledda.is • kk*

3 Hótel Hallormstaður

Cosy country hotel inside Iceland's most extensive forest, close to Lögurinn lake. The hotel has self-contained wooden cottages, rooms in a large guesthouse and summer-only accommodation with a geothermal pool at the school nearby. *Map G3 • Hallormstaður, near Egilsstaðir • 471 2400 • www.hotel701.is • k–kk*

4 Fosshótel Vatnajökull

Functional, tidy place, with warm but small and simply furnished rooms that have breakfast included in the price. Given the location, pay extra to get a room with glacier views. Popular stopover for large tour groups. *Map G5 • Route 1 near Höfn, Hornafjörður • 478 2555 • www.fosshotel.is • kkk*

5 Hólar í Hjaltadal

Site of a historically important cathedral, the island's largest estate and Hólar University, which opens its student accommodation to tourists during the summer months. Call in advance to check room availability and facilities. *Map D2 • Hólar, near Sauðárkrókur • 849 6348 • Jun–Aug only • booking@holar.is • kk*

6 Edda Hótel Skógar

Storm-proof building close to one of Iceland's most impressive waterfalls, the eccentric Skógar Museum and superb hiking trail to Þórsmörk. Plain, serviceable rooms with shared facilities, sleeping-bag space and a restaurant. *Map D6 • Skógar • 444 4830 • 10 Jun–25 Aug • www.hoteledda.is • kk*

7 Edda Hótel Vík

This Edda hotel is classier than most, with *en suite* doubles in the main building and self-contained wooden cabins on the grassy slopes at the rear. Breakfast is served in the lobby; head to Vík for your other meals. *Map D6 • Route 1, Vík í Mýrdal • 444 4840 • May–Sep • www.hoteledda.is • kk*

8 Edda Hótel Nesjum

Well-placed for glacier trips to Vatnajökull or hiking in the Lónsöræfi Reserve, these school buildings offer straight-forward doubles and dorms with shared washrooms and toilets, plus a restaurant known for its evening buffets. *Map G5 • Höfn • 444 4850 • 10 Jun–20 Aug • www.hoteledda.is • kk*

9 Edda Hótel ML Laugarvatn

One of two Eddas in town, this huge complex offers doubles with either *en suite* or shared facilities and an in-house restaurant. It is close to the Golden Circle attractions, a huge pool and Laugarvatn lake. *Map C5 • Laugarvatn • 444 4810 • www.hoteledda.is • kkk*

10 Edda Hótel Ísafjörður

Near Ísafjörður's centre, this school (for most of the year) has good facilities. Rooms have *en suite* or shared bathrooms and sleeping-bag space in the heated sports hall or tent pitches. You will have to eat in town. *Map B2 • Torfsnes, Ísafjörður • 444 4960 • 14 Jun–20 Aug • www.hoteledda.is • kkk*

Many boarding schools in Iceland operate as hotels during the summer under the Edda Hótel banner.

Above **Reykjavík Campsite**

Price Categories

For a standard double room per night (with breakfast if included), taxes and extra charges.	
k	under ISK10,000
kk	ISK10,000–20,000
kkk	ISK20,000–30,000
kkkk	ISK30,000–40,000
kkkkk	over ISK40,000

TOP 10 Character Stays and Campsites

1 Hótel Laki

Converted farmhouse with smart *en suite* doubles in the main building and self-contained cabins suited for groups alongside. It is located on the edge of a huge pseudocrater and lava field stretching north up to Lakagígar. *Map E5 • Efri Vík, Kirkjubæjarklaustur • 487 4694 • www.hotellaki.is • kkk*

2 Hótel Látrabjarg

Originally a boarding school, this cosy hotel has a great location, close to the beach and bird cliffs. Rooms have *en suite* or shared facilities. Freshwater trout fishing and horse rental available. *Map A2 • Near Route 612/615 junction, Patreksfjörður • 825 0025, 456 1500 • Mid-May–Sep • www.latrabjarg.com • kkkk*

3 Hótel Anna

Great rural location with the white mass of Eyjafjallajökull rising above. Large beds, low ceilings and old wooden furniture add character to the red-roofed farmhouse. Price includes buffet breakfast and use of hot tubs and sauna. *Map D6 • Moldnúpur, Route 246, between Skógar and Seljarlandsfoss • 487 8950, 899 5955 • 1 Apr–1 Nov • www.hotelanna.is • kkk*

4 Hótel Tindastól

Iceland's oldest hotel, in business since 1884, even hosting Marlene Dietrich, who was here during World War II to entertain US troops. A fantastic wooden building with a flagstoned outdoor spa and resident ghost adding to the atmosphere. *Map D2 • Lindargata 3, Sauðárkrókur • 453 5002 • www.hoteltindastoll.com • kkk*

5 Reykjavík Campsite

The huge grassy slope has room for hundreds of tents, near Laugardalur's swimming pool, stadium and botanical gardens. A 20-minute walk from the city centre, the campsite has a covered cooking area, toilets and showers. *Map R2 • Sundlaugarvegur 32, 104 Reykjavík • 568 6944 • www.reykjavikcampsite.is • kk*

6 Hótel Dyrhólaey Brekkur

Lakeside farmstead up in the hills above Dyrholaey bird reserve. Clean, warm and comfortable rooms with private bathrooms; some have views of the Mýrdalsjökull icecap. Staff are helpful and the restaurant has a good-value evening buffet. *Map D6 • Near Vík • 487 1333 • www.dyrholaey.is • kk*

7 Hlíð Campsite

Great place to base yourself while at Mývatn; tent pitches have superb views over Reykjahlíð and the lake, with hot showers, toilets and outdoor sinks for laundry or washing up. Wooden cabins and dorm building available if you do not have a tent. *Map F2 • Reykjahlíð, Mývatn • 464 4103 • www.myvatnaccommodation.is • kk*

8 Hamrar Campsite

Enormous camping grounds near woodland outside of Akureyri; you do not need to reserve a space in advance. There are toilets, free hot showers, washing machines and tumble dryers on-site, along with a kitchen and covered dining area. *Map E2 • Kjarnaskógur, Akureyri • 843 0002 • www.hamrar.is • kk*

9 Egilsstaðir Campsite

Scruffy and occasionally boggy camping ground with some sheltered woody patches near Egilsstaðir's tourist information and long-distance bus stop; you need to choose your site carefully. Good shower and toilet facilities and a tiny, sheltered barbecue and seating area. *Map G3 • Egilsstaðir • 471 2320 • www.east.is • kk*

10 Galtalækur II

Self-contained cabins or campsite near Hekla volcano and Tangavatn lake – you can buy fishing licenses here. Visit the nearby Þjófafoss waterfall. *Map C5 • Galtalækur II, Route 26, Rangárþing ýtra, Hella • 487 6528 • galtalaekur2@simnet.is • kk*

More farmstays at www.farmholidays.is

General Index

Acknowledgments

The Author
David Leffman is a travel writer and photographer who first visited Iceland in 1981. Apart from *Top 10 Iceland*, he has authored *Eyewitness China* for Dorling Kindersley, along with guidebooks to Iceland, Australia, Indonesia, China and Hong Kong for Rough Guides. He has also led specialist guided tours to China.

Photographer Nigel Hicks
Additional Photography Peter Gathercole, Steve Gorton, Rough Guides/David Leffman, Clive Streeter
Contents Outline Michael Kissane
Streetsmart Author (pp118–127) Laura Dixon
Fact Checker and Phrase Book Compiler Bergljót Njóla Jakobsdóttir

At DK INDIA
Managing Editor Aruna Ghose
Editorial Manger Sheeba Bhatnagar
Design Manager Kavita Saha
Project Editor Shikha Kulkarni
Project Designers Namrata Adhwaryu, Shruti Singhi
Assistant Cartographic Manager Suresh Kumar
Cartographer Zafar-ul-Islam Khan
Senior Picture Research Coordinator Taiyaba Khatoon
Picture Researcher Sumita Khatwani
DTP Coordinator Azeem Siddiqui
DTP Designer Rakesh Kumar
Proofreader and Indexer Andy Kulkarni

At DK LONDON
Publisher Douglas Amrine
List Manager Christine Stroyan
Design Manager Mabel Chan
Senior Editor Sadie Smith
Cartographer Stuart James
DTP Operator Jason Little
Production Controller Danielle Smith
Revisions Team
Ashwin Raju Adimari, Barbara Balfour, Marta Bescos, Fay Franklin, Bharti Karakoti, Priyanka Kumar, Nicola Malone, Alison McGill, Ellen Root, Susana Smith, Ajay Verma

Picture Credits
Key: a-above; b-below/bottom; c-centre; f-far; l-left; r-right; t-top.

Photography Permissions
Dorling Kindersley would like to thank the following for their assistance and kind permission to photograph at their establishments:

Þjóðminjasafn Íslands/The National Museum of Iceland; Akranes Museum; B5 Bar, Reykjavík; The Blue Lagoon; Búðir Hótel; Café Paris; The Culture House - National Centre for Cultural Heritage; The Dubliner Pub, Reykavík; Emigration Centre; The Fish Market Restaurant; Fjalakotturinn; Fríða Frænka; Gallery Restaurant, Hótel Gígur; Hótel Holt; Hornið; The Húsavík Whale Museum; Icelandic Fish & Chips; Hótel Ísafjörður; Jarðböðin Nature Baths; Jómfrúin; Osvur Museum; Hótel Plaza; Þrír Frakkar; Radisson SAS Saga Hótel; The Reykjavík Art Museum; The Reykjavík Art Museum Kjarvalsstaðir; Sævar Karl; Settlement Centre; Sigríðustofa; Sigurjón Ólafsson Museum; Skógar Museum; The Visitor Centre's Souvenir shop; Vox Restaurant. Also, all the other churches, museums, hotels, restaurants, shops, galleries and other sights are too numerous to thank individually.

The publisher would like to thank the following individuals, companies, and picture libraries for their kind permission to reproduce their photographs:

4CORNERS IMAGES: SIME/ Giovanni Simeone 28-29

ALAMY: Arctic Images 54br, 65cl, 101cl, Ragnar Th Sigurdsson 45tr, Robert Harding Picture Library/ Patrik Dieudonne 15bc; Ian Bottle 100tr; Phil Degginger 26cla; Bragi Josefsson 60tr; Juniors Bildarchiv 46tc; Wolfgang Kaehler 68-69; Nordicphotos 98tr; North Wind Picture Archives 30tr; Bjarki Reyr MR 82tr; S.I.N. 55tr; Frantisek Staud 116-117; Haraldur Stefansson 54t, 55tl; Clive Tully 16cb

HÓTEL ALDAN: 132tl

BÚRIÐ: 75tr

CORBIS: Arctic-Images 27tl; Hans Strand 38bl

GETTY IMAGES: U. Baumgarten 119tr

GÖTUBARINN: 44tl

HARPA REYKJAVÍK CONCERT HALL AND CONFERENCE CENTRE: Bára Kristindóttir 70cl

LAUNDROMAT CAFÉ: 42bl
LEBOWSKI BAR: 45tr

MARY EVANS PICTURE LIBRARY: 30cl

NATUREPL.COM: Wild Wonders of Europe / O Haarberg 34br

PHOTOLIBRARY: age fotostock/ Jose Fuste Raga 4-5, 84-85; N A Callow 104-105; Imagebroker.net / Christian Handl 11bc, /Dr Torsten Heydenreich 16-17c, 22-23c; Lonely Planet Images/ Grant Dixon 19cb; Nordic Photos/ Inger Helene Boasson 53tl, /Kristjan Maack 48-49, 51cl, /Sigurge ir Sigurjonsson 102tr; Oxford Scientific (OSF)/ Richard Packwood 7tl, 102tl; Photononstop/ Philippe Crochet 28-29

PHOTOSHOT: 19tl; Bryan & Cherry Alexander 94tr

SUNNA GUESTHOUSE: 131tl
All other images are © Dorling Kindersley. For further information see *www.dkimages.com*

Special Editions of DK Travel Guides

DK Travel Guides can be purchased in bulk quantities at discounted prices for use in promotions or as premiums. We are also able to offer special editions and personalized jackets, corporate imprints, and excerpts from all of our books, tailored specifically to meet your own needs.

To find out more, please contact:

(in the United States) **SpecialSales@dk.com**

(in the UK) **travelspecialsales@uk.dk.com**

(in Canada) DK Special Sales at **general@tourmaline.ca**

(in Australia) **business.development@pearson.com.au**

Phrase Book

Icelandic belongs to the Nordic family of languages. Many sounds in Icelandic do not exist in English, so the pronunciations given below are for guidance only. Icelandic has three letters in the alphabet that do not exist in modern English: þ (called "thorn", pronounced th as in "thin"); ð ("eth", pronounced as soft th as in "the"); æ ("aye", pronounced as i as in "light"). Stress falls on the first syllable of the word.

Guidelines for Pronunciation

Vowels

There are 7 vowels – a, e, i, o, u, y and æ, 5 of which take a stress accent, which changes the pronunciation. The "o" can have an umlaut over it.

a = as in sat
á = ow as in owl
e = as in met
i = as in sit
í = as in feel
o = as in hot
ó = as in hole
ö = "uh" sound
u = as in put
ú = as in fool
ý = ee as in meet
æ = i as in light

Letter combinations

Some combined letters in Icelandic have special pronunciations.
fl = as pl
fn = as p
ll = as in tl
sj = as in sh in fish
ng = as nk at the end of a word and ng in the middle
ey = as a in hail
ei = as a in hail
au = as o in hole

In an Emergency

Help!	Hjálp!	hy-oulp
Call a doctor	Náið lækni	nou-ith ee laek-ni
Call an ambulance	Hringdu í sjúkrabíl	hreen-du ee syoo-kra-beel
Call the police	Hringdu í lögregluna	hreen-du ee leu-rekl-una
Call the fire brigade	Hringdu í slökkviliðið	hreen-du ee sleuk-vi-lith-ith

Communication Essentials

Yes	Já	y**o**w
No	Nei	n**ay**
Please (offering)	Gjörðu svo vel	gy**eu**rth-**u** sv**o** vel
Thank you	Takk/takk fyrir	t**a**kk /t**a**kk f**i**r-ir
Excuse me	Afsakið	**a**f-sak-ith
Hello	Halló	h**a**llo
Hello (polite)	Vertu sæl/sæll	v**e**rt-u s**ae**l(f.)/ s**ae**tl (m.)
Goodbye	Bless	bl**e**ss
Good night	Góða nótt	g**o**-tha n**o**tt
morning	Góðan morgunn	g**o**-than m**o**rg-un
evening	Gott kvöld	g**o**tt kv**eu**-ld

Useful Phrases

How are you?	Hvað segirðu gott?	kv**ah**th s**ay**-irth-u g**o**tt
Very well, thank you.	Allt gott	**a**lht g**o**tt
That's fine.	Það er fínt/gott	th**a**th **e**r f**ee**n-t/ gott
Where is/ are …?	Hvar er/eru …?	kv**a**r **e**r/**e**ru
How do I get to …?	Hvernig kemst ég til …?	kv**e**rn-ig k**e**m-st y**ie**g t**i**l
Do you speak English?	Talarðu ensku?	t**a**l-arth-u **e**nsk-u
I don't understand.	Ég skil ekki	y**ie**g sk**i**l **e**kki

Shopping

How much does this cost?	Hvað kostar þetta?	kv**a**th k**o**st-ar th**e**tt-a
I would like …	Ég ætla að fá …	y**ie**g **ae**tla **a**th f**ou**
Do you take credit cards?	Takið þið kreditkort?	t**a**k-ith th**i**th kr**e**-dit-k**o**rt
Do you take traveller's cheques?	Takið þið ferðatékka?	t**a**k-ith th**i**th f**e**rth-a-t**ie**kk-a
What time do you open?	Hvenær opnið þið/lokið þið?	kv**e**n-aer **o**ph-nith/l**o**k-ith th**i**th
this one	þessi hérna	th**e**si h**ie**r-nah
that one	þessi þarna	th**e**si th**a**r-nah
expensive	dýrt	d**ee**r-t
size	stærð	sd**ae**rth

Types of Shops

bakery	bakarí	b**a**-ka-ree
bank	banki	b**ou**n-ki
chemist	apótek	**a**p-o-tek
fishmonger	fiskibúð	f**i**sk-i-b**oo**th
garage (mechanics)	bílaverkstæði	b**ee**l-a-v**e**rk-staeth-i
market	markaður	m**a**rk-ath-ur
post office	pósthús	p**o**st-hoos
supermarket	matarverslun	m**ah**-dar-v**e**rs-lun
travel agent	ferðaskrifstofa	f**e**rth-a-skr**i**f-sdofa

Sightseeing

art gallery	listagallerí	l**i**st-ah-g**a**ll-er-ee
bay	flói	fl**o**-i
beach	fjara	fy**a**r-ah
bike	reiðhjól	r**ai**th-hyeeol
bus (town)	strætó	str**ae**h-tou
bus (long dist)	rúta	r**oo**-ta
bus station	umferðami-ðstöð	**u**m-fertha-mi**th**-steuth
bus ticket	strætó/rútu miði	str**ae**h-tou/ r**oo**-tu m**i**thi
car	bíll	b**ee**-dlh
car rental	bílaleiga	b**ee**lah-l**ai**g-a
cathedral	dómkirkja	d**o**m-kirk-ya
church	kirkja	k**i**rk-ya
glacier	jökull	y**eu**-kudl
harbour	höfn	h**eu**bn
hot spring	hver	kv**e**r
island	eyja	**ai**-yah
lake	stöðuvatn	st**eu**-thu-vatn
mountain	fjall	f**ya**dlh
museum	safn	s**a**bn
tourist information	upplýsinga-miðstöð	**u**ph-lees-eenga-m**i**th-sdeuth
waterfall	foss	f**o**ss

Staying in a Hotel

Do you have a vacant room?	Eigið þið laust herbergi?	**ai**gith th**i**th l**ao**st h**e**r-berg-i
double room with double bed	Tveggja manna herbergi með hjónarúmmi	tv**e**gg-ya-m**a**nn-a h**er**-berg-i m**e**th hy**o**n-ah-r**oo**m-i
twin room	tveggja manna herbergi	tv**e**gg-ya m**a**nn-a h**e**r-berg-i
single room	eins manns herbergi	**ay**ns m**a**nns h**e**r-berg-i
room with bath	herbergi með baði	h**e**r-berg-i m**e**th b**a**th-i
shower	sturta	st**u**rh-tah
I have a reservation	Ég á pantað	yi**e**g **ou** p**a**nt-ath

Eating Out

Have you got a table?	Eigið þið laust borð?	**aig**ith th**i**th l**ao**st b**o**rth
I'd like to reserve a table	Gæti ég pantað borð	gy**ae**t-i yi**e**g p**a**nt-ath b**o**rth
breakfast	morgunmatur	m**o**rg-un-mat-ur
lunch	hádegismatur	h**ou**-deg-is-mat-ur
dinner	kvöldmatur	kv**eu**ld-mat-ur
The bill, please	Gæti ég fengið reikninginn, takk fyrir inn	gy**ae**t-i yi**e**g f**e**ng-ith r**ai**kn-ing-t**a**kk f**i**r-ir
waitress/waiter	þjónn	thy**o**-dn
menu	matseðill	m**ah**t-seth-idl
starter	smáréttur	sm**ou**-riet-ur
first course	forréttur	f**o**r-riet-ur
main course	aðalréttur	**a**thal-riet-ur
dessert	eftirréttur	**e**ft-ir-riet-ur
wine list	vínlisti	v**ee**n-list-i
glass	glas	glas
bottle	flaska	fl**a**sk-a
knife	hnífur	hn**ee**v-ur
fork	gaffall	g**a**ff-adl
spoon	skeið	skaith

Menu Decoder

bjór	byorh	beer
brauð	br**ao**th	bread
ferskir ávextir irh	f**e**rsk-ir **ou**-vekst	fresh fruit
fiskur	f**i**sk-ur	fish
franskar kartöflur	fr**a**nsk-ar k**a**rt-eufl-ur	chips
grænmeti	gr**ae**n-met-i	vegetables
grillað	gr**i**ll-ath	grilled
gufusoðið	g**u**-vu-soth-ith	poached
hvítvín	kv**ee**t-veen	white wine
ís	ees	ice cream
kaka/vínarbrauð	c**a**-ka/v**ee**n-ar-braoth	cake, pastry
kartöflur	k**a**rt-eufl-ur	potatoes
kjöt	kyeut	meat
kjúklingur	ky**oo**k-leeng-ur	chicken
lamb	lambh	lamb
laukur	l**ao**k-ur	onions
lax	laks	salmon
mjólk	myulk	milk
nautakjöt	n**ao**-ta-staik	beef
ostur	**o**s-tur	cheese
pipar	ph**i**-par	pepper
pylsa or pulsa	p**i**ls-ah/p**u**l-sah	hotdog
rauðvín	r**ao**th-veen	red wine
rækjur	r**ai**-kyur	prawns
sjávarréttur	sy**ou**-var-r**ie**td-ur	seafood
smjör	smyeurh	butter
soðið	s**o**th-ith	boiled
sódavatn	s**o**-da-vadn	mineral water
sósa	s**o**-sa	sauce
steikt	staikt	fried
súkkulaði	s**oo**k-u-lath-i	chocolate
súpa	s**oo**-ba	soup
svínakjöt	sv**ee**n-a-kyeut	pork
sykur	s**ii**k-ur	sugar
te	teh	tea
vatn	vahdn	water
ýsa	**ee**-sa	haddock

Numbers

1	einn	aydn
2	tveir	tvayr
3	þrír	threer
4	fjórir	fy**o**r-ir
5	fimm	fim
6	sex	segs
7	sjö	syeu
8	átta	**ou**tt-a
9	níu	n**ee**-u
10	tíu	t**ee**-u
11	ellefu	**e**dl-ev-u
12	tólf	tolvh
13	þrettán	thr**e**tt-dyoun
14	fjórtán	fy**o**rh-dyoun
15	fimmtán	f**i**m-dyoun
16	sextán	s**e**gs- dyoun
17	sautján	s**ao**-dyoun
18	átján	**ou**t-dyoun
19	nítján	n**ee**-dyoun
20	tuttugu	t**u**tt-ug-u
21	tuttugu og einn	t**u**tt-ug-u og **ay**dn
30	þrjátíu	thry**ou**-tee-u
40	fjörtíu	fy**eu**r-u-tee-u
50	fimmtíu	f**i**m-tee-u
60	sextíu	s**e**gs-tee-u
70	sjötíu	sy**eu**-tee-u
80	áttatíu	**ou**tt-a-tee-u
90	níutíu	n**ee**-u-tee-u
100	hundrað	h**u**nd-rath
1000	þúsund	th**oo**s-und
1,000,000	miljón	m**i**l-ee-yon

Time

one minute	ein mínúta	**ay**n m**ee**n-oot-a
one hour	ein klukkustund	**ay**n kl**u**k-u-stun-dh
a day	dagur	d**a**g-ur
Monday	mánudagur	m**ou**n-u-dag-ur
Tuesday	þriðjudagur	thr**i**th-yu-dag-ur
Wednesday	miðvikudagur	m**i**th-vik-u-dag-ur
Thursday	fimmtudagur	f**i**mt-u-dag-ur
Friday	föstudagur	f**eu**st-u-dag-ur
Saturday	laugardagur	l**ao**g-ar-dag-ur
Sunday	sunnudagur	s**u**nnu-dag-ur

Useful Signs

campsite	tjaldsvæði	ty**a**ld-svaethi
closed	lokað	l**oh**k-ath
danger	hætta	h**ae**tt-ah
end of bitumen/tarmac	malbik/bundið slitlag endar	m**a**l-bik/b**u**n-dith sl**i**t-lag **e**nd-ar
exit	út/útgangur	**oo**t/**oo**t-goung-ur
entry	inn/inngangur	**i**nn/**I**nn-goung-ur
forbidden	bannað	b**a**nn-ath
gents toilets	karlaklósett	k**a**rl-a cl**o**-sett
jeep track	jeppaslóð	y**e**pp-ah-sloth
ladies toilets	kvennaklósett	kv**e**nn-a-cl**o**-sett
open	opið	**o**p-ith
parking	bílastæði	b**ee**-la-st**ae**th-i
one-lane bridge	einbreið brú	**ay**n-braith br**oo**
toilet	klósett	cl**o**-sett

Iceland Town Index

Reykjavík Selected Street Index